THE WORLD OF
PRO HOCKEY

Dedication
To Irv, Sandy and Cori – my three very best friends; and to
partner Bruce for the reference.

Acknowledgements
In piecing together the fragments of my very first book, I would
like to acknowledge the invaluable assistance I received from
some of the finest people I've ever had the privilege of working
with.

First and foremost, I'd like to thank both Hanni Edmonds and
Trevor Hall, who not only showed confidence in a total stranger's
ability to handle this assignment, but who also contributed so
immeasurably to the success of this venture with their
cooperation and flexibility.

A special note of gratitude to Winnipeg Jets' publicity director
Ralph Carter for his much-appreciated gesture of hospitality
during the Smythe Division playoff final against Edmonton, and
for his superb work in conjunction with fellow P.R. directors
Gerry Helper (Buffalo), Bill Jamieson (Detroit) and Bill Tuele
(Edmonton) during the Stanley Cup Finals.

Thanks also to John Halligan, Dan Leary and Gary Meagher
of the NHL for their efforts in the same series, and to the
victorious Edmonton coach Glen Sather for that round of drinks
at the Empress of China.

To the NHL beat writers who offered me their valuable
perceptiveness, I extend my warmest appreciation – most
sincerely, to Frank Orr of the *Toronto Star*, for the special kind of
insight only he possesses. And finally, thanks to Norma and Phil
for keeping me company during those long, lonely nights in
Winnipeg.
Happy Reading

Howard Berger,
Toronto,
June, 1985.

THE WORLD OF
PRO HOCKEY

Text by
Howard Berger

Photography by
Bruce Bennett
& Brian Winkler

CRESCENT BOOKS
NEW YORK

FOREWORD

Let me introduce myself. I am Larry Robinson, of the Montreal Canadiens of the National Hockey League. I am very pleased to have been asked to write a few words for readers — and particularly young readers — of this fabulous new hockey book. I am convinced that you will find among its colourful pages some fascinating facts, and some spectacular pictures of a much-loved game, and that it will give you many hours of fantastic reading and enjoyment.

As a veteran defenceman who has played thirteen seasons in the NHL, I consider myself very lucky to have been drafted by a super organization — the Montreal Canadiens. I will never forget how stunned and surprised I was when in the 1971 amateur draft I was claimed by the Montreal Hockey Club as its fourth pick. From then on, it was a dream come true! After a few seasons with the Nova Scotia Voyageurs of the American Hockey League, I was called up by Mr. Sam Pollock, the general manager of Les Canadiens, and soon became a regular defenceman.

What memories I cherish of my long professional career! There was the spine-tingling thrill of my very first Stanley Cup; my first game, ending in a 3-3 tie, against the Soviet Red Army team — the best game I ever played in; my two Conn Smythe trophies as the Most Valued Player of the Stanley Cup play-offs; the many tremendous seasons when I played with Serge Savard and Guy Lapointe, which earned us the Press nickname of the "Big Three" of professional hockey.

I consider myself very lucky to have made it this far in hockey. I often compare minor and amateur hockey to a funnel. The top of the funnel is full of hockey players all eager to make it to the professionals. The bottom part is the small opening where a few lucky ones make it through.

You know, if you are a beginner, or a regular amateur hockey player, there are a few things you should never forget. Hockey teaches you discipline, and gives you a formation in life. Whatever happens in your careers, you should be thankful to have played the game. You should always be thankful to your parents, who took you to the rinks for practices, and to those dedicated minor league coaches that have taught you the game. I am enormously grateful to my parents, my family, my coaches at all levels of the game, because without them, it would have been impossible to experience the thirteen wonderful years of my life devoted to the sport I love most of all... Hockey.

Good reading. Good luck!

Sincerely,

Larry Robinson

SPEED, STYLE, AND OIL ON ICE
Hockey in the 1980s

Professors of hockey wisdom from coast to coast in North America often expound that the current-day game is predicated, typically, on speed, grace and rapid puck movement. While this oft-repeated statement has its merits, it could be deemed something of an affront to the Edmonton Oilers – a hockey club that has prodigiously cornered the market in all three areas.

Thanks to an astute front-office staff with contemporary ideas, and the glaring presence of at least one superstar player at every position, the Oilers display these components brilliantly, timelessly and *most* exclusively. The propensity, therefore, to suggest that hockey in general has gone this route, is both inaccurate and presumptuous. The elements of an explosive and persistent attack – including superior coaching methods and playing personnel – belong solely to the Edmonton Oilers and the kudos must follow in accordance.

There simply is no other team in the National Hockey League, or arguably in the world, quite like the Oilers. Both speed and puck movement have been refined beyond comparison by the two-time defending Stanley Cup champions, who have set a standard for which every team can aim. Several NHL clubs appear to be following Edmonton's resourceful path and may, eventually, devise a system to dethrone the champs. Until that day arrives, however, the Oilers should remain in a class by themselves.

This revolution, of sorts, did not happen by accident. As part of the four-team merger of World Hockey Association teams in 1979-80, the Oilers joined the NHL with a master plan, and the club has carried it out to astonishing heights. Ironically, the WHA is both credited with pioneering the modern-day vogue, and implicated for inducing the diluted quality of professional hockey that preceded it.

In their Stanley Cup years of 1974 and 1975, the Philadelphia Flyers, for example, took advantage of an era during which the overall talent pool dwindled amidst the inhabitance of 32 big-league teams. With 18 clubs in the NHL, and 14 more in the WHA, there simply were not enough quality players around to stock the aggregation. As a result, both leagues were forced to supplement their rosters with dismal, second-rate performers who would otherwise have been destined for minor-league employment.

A goodly number in this group were fraught with severe deficiencies in the basic skill areas – skating, passing, shooting – and many turned to aggression as a form of big-league survival. Philadelphia coach Fred Shero adapted foremost to the general depreciation of talent by invoking a system based, extensively, on intimidation and abrasiveness. As a result, mediocre players like Dave Schultz, Bob Kelly, Don Saleski and Andre Dupont enacted key roles in the two Stanley Cup triumphs.

Lest we forget, Philadelphia's sizeable contingent of quality players – Bobby Clarke, Reg Leach, Bill Barber, Jimmy Watson, Rick MacLeish and Bernie Parent (the best goalie in the world back then) – was the *actual* prime mover behind the club's fortunes. The Clarke-Leach-Barber forward unit was as potent as any line in the NHL. But many so-called hockey experts chose to credit the intimidation factor, by itself, for Philadelphia's prosperity. In hindsight, this proved to be a rather grave error and it retarded the subsequent maturation of several NHL teams – most notably, Toronto, Pittsburgh, and Detroit – which imprudently chose to focus on the roughhouse tactics of the Flyer system by seeking brawn over brains.

Not until the final years of the WHA did anyone bother to realize the positive effect it was beginning to exert on the game. Thanks to a penchant for recruiting skilled European-born players, the Winnipeg Jets gradually became the most exciting and innovative team in either league. A pair of Swedish-born forwards – center Ulf Nilsson and right-winger Anders Hedberg – teamed with the immortal Bobby Hull to form what many observers have called the greatest forward unit of all time. Instead of adhering to the conventional "up-and-down" style of play, with the wingers watching their side of the ice and the center-man looking after the middle, this threesome meandered and criss-crossed in the neutral zone, using both its individual and collective speed and passing skill to confuse opposing checkers. Adding a critical component to this unique system was a proverbial "fourth forward" in the person of fellow-Swede Lars-Erik Sjoberg – a swift, agile defenceman who could keep pace with the speedy forwards and advance the puck into the offensive zone. The result was an explosive and diversified attack – first made famous, in North America, by the Soviet Union national team.

Lured to the NHL by the big bucks of Sonny Werblin in New York, Hedberg and Nilsson defected to the Rangers for the 1978-79 season – the final year of the WHA. In November of that season, the Indianapolis Racers and Edmonton Oilers completed a straight business transaction that would soon rank among the most profound and magnanimous deals in hockey history.

Vancouver entrepreneur Nelson Skalbania – owner of the Indianapolis team – had robbed the junior hockey cradle in Canada the previous May by signing 17-year-old scoring sensation Wayne Gretzky, of the Sault Ste. Marie Greyhounds, to a personal-services contract. Indianapolis fans, who had never before heard of Gretzky, were indifferent towards the blond, skinny kid and the team in general. With a feeble season-ticket count, Skalbania decided to look for someone to purchase Gretzky's contract and he immediately found two prospective buyers in Michael Gobuty of Winnipeg and Edmonton's Peter Pocklington. According to the now-famous yarn, Gretzky, Gobuty and Pocklington boarded a private plane in Indianapolis – not knowing where it might land – and the two business tycoons presented their offers to The Kid. Somewhere high above the clouds, Gretzky accepted Pocklington's proposal and the plane proceeded to Edmonton. The Brantford, Ont, native went on to finish third in WHA scoring with 110 points (including 46 goals) and the Oilers joined the NHL the following season with a distinct plan for success.

"We saw what Winnipeg accomplished with its European influence during the final years of the WHA and we realized that team speed and puck movement were the new avenues for the NHL," recalls Barry Fraser – Edmonton's current-day director of player personnel and the club's chief scout back then. "In order to become competitive quickly, we decided to acquire mobile players who could skate well and handle the puck with authority. The entire system, however, was based around Gretzky. His amazing puck-handling and passing skill was obvious from the moment he first joined us. If not for his presence, we might have gone a different route altogether."

With firm direction from general manager/coach Glen Sather, shrewd and thorough work from Fraser's scouting staff on both sides of the big pond, and a little bit of luck, the Oilers began meticulously to assemble all the necessary ingredients of a championship team. The following is a brief chronology of Edmonton's adroit acquisitions, and the retrospective oversights made by other NHL teams:

1979 – The Oilers "lucked out" on two players who would become mainstays on their path to the Stanley Cup. Forwards Mark Messier and Glenn Anderson were selected in the second and third rounds respectively of the amateur draft, and Fraser still pinches himself when he considers the stupendous results.

"Mark played for Cincinnati and Indianapolis of the WHA when he was 17 years old and he only scored one goal in 52 games," Fraser remembers. "But he had a good combination of speed and strength that we felt would suit our system when he matured. We saw Glenn play at the University of Denver in 1978-79 but they dropped him from the team that season because his scholastic marks weren't up to par. In the summertime, we watched him work out with the Canadian Olympic team, alongside guys like Laurie Boschman and Paul MacLean. And he was right up there with both of them. I think we got a little lucky because not too many other scouts bothered to notice him. We liked Glenn right away, although we didn't know much about him."

Rob Ramage, Perry Turnbull and Mike Foligno were the top three selections in the '79 draft. Messier went to the Oilers in the third round, 48th overall, behind the likes of Ray Allison, Jimmy Mann, Mike Perovich, Errol Rausse, Tim Trimper, Dean Hopkins and Boris Fistric (if you're thinking "Who?", you're not alone). Edmonton then drafted Anderson, 69th overall. Players selected in-between Messier and Anderson included such notables as Bennett Wolf, Bill Whelton, Steve Peters and Harvie Pocza. Incredible, when you think of it! The Oilers had earlier selected defenceman Kevin Lowe of the Quebec Remparts, 21st overall. Just prior to training camp, Sather inked defenceman Charlie Huddy – an Oshawa Generals grad – to a free-agent contract.

Edmonton made the playoffs in its initial NHL season, only to be swept by the Philadelphia Flyers in the best-of-five preliminary round. But the Oilers went down fighting against the regular-season champions, losing the first and third games in overtime.

1980 – If the Oilers appeared ingenious for their '79 acquisitions, they would take on the aura of immortality the following year. The 1980 amateur draft landed Edmonton two players who would establish themselves, before long, as the very best in the game at their positions.

The first selection (6th overall) was a popular one, as all 21 teams rated Kitchener Ranger defenceman Paul Coffey near the top of their lists. He had compiled 102 points in 75 games with the Soo and Kitchener during the 1979-80 campaign, and the Oilers figured he would develop into the wheelhorse they required along the blueline. Doug Wickenheiser (Montreal), David Babych (Winnipeg), Denis Savard (Chicago), Larry Murphy (Los Angeles), and Darren Veitch (Washington) went ahead of him. "We figured Paul would be weak defensively, coming out of junior, but he had all the offensive polish in the world and we were more than willing to be patient with him," Fraser says.

After making winger Shawn Babcock of the Windsor Spitfires its second choice in the draft, Edmonton stunned the rest of the league with its third claim. During the final season of the WHA, the Oilers travelled to Finland for a series of exhibition games against first-division teams. A 19-year-old Finnish winger – Jari Kurri – had impressed a wealth of NHL scouts with his superb performances in the 1979 World Junior Hockey Championships, and he continued to fascinate the Oiler brass during the club's European visit. Kurri had all the prerequisites of a high first-round draft choice, except one: availability.

In anticipation of the 1981 World Hockey Championships – at Helsinki – practically all native players were re-signing two-year commitments with the Finnish national team and it was generally understood that Kurri would follow suit. With a burning desire, though, to test his talents in the NHL, Kurri hesitated in promising his services to the national squad and Fraser became privy to this esoteric information via his lavish network of reliable contacts in Finland. Kurri's agent, Don Baizley – who had negotiated the WHA contracts of Anders Hedberg and Ulf Nilsson with the Jets – informed his client that both Edmonton and Winnipeg were NHL possibilities. But the Jet sources regarding Kurri's status in Finland weren't quite as dependable as Fraser's, and Winnipeg decided not to risk a high draft choice on a player it might not have prompt access to.

With the other 19 teams under the assumption Kurri would remain in Finland, he was still available midway through the fourth round. When the Oilers selected him, 69th overall, about 200 chins dropped in bewilderment. For the sake of posterity, a brief list of prospects chosen ahead of Kurri included such attractions as Joe Ward, Len Dawes, John Newberry, Paul Mercier and Jay Miller. Once again... incredible.

One further bit of business saw the Oilers select goaltender Andy Moog from Billings of the Western Hockey League in the seventh round, 132nd overall. Mike Braun and Frank Perkins were the two stiffs chosen directly before him.

With a splendid foundation of youth and speed, the Oilers took their first official step towards glory when they executed a shocking first-round playoff sweep of the Montreal Canadiens – who had merely won four Stanley Cups in the previous six years. Thanks, mainly, to a marvellous performance by Moog, the Oilers then extended the defending-champion New York Islanders to a gruelling six-game quarterfinal series, before bowing out.

1981 – Buoyed by Moog's unforeseen heroics, the Oilers decided to team him with a youthful partner and form a reliable goaltending tandem. Dave Dryden, Eddie Mio, Ron Low, Jim Corsi and Don Cutts had adequately split the netminding chores throughout Edmonton's first two NHL seasons, but the Oiler brass recognized the obvious need for greater quality and stability at that critical position. As a result, the Oilers opted for the highest-rated goalie in the '81 amateur draft by selecting Victoria Cougars' netminder Grant Fuhr, 8th overall. In doing so, they declined opportunities to upgrade both their scoring potential and defensive mobility by passing up Oshawa Generals' winger Tony Tanti (who had surpassed Gretzky's OHL record for most goals in a season) and hard-shooting defenceman Allan MacInnis – Coffey's ex-teammate in Kitchener. Edmonton missed yet another chance to draft a mobile rearguard later on, when it overlooked American-born Chris Chelios in favor of Regina Pats' winger Todd Strueby.

Late in the 1981-82 season, the Oilers acquired center Laurie Boschman from Toronto in exchange for minor-league left-winger Walt Poddubny. Boschman had been Toronto's first-round draft choice in 1979, but Leaf owner Harold Ballard disdained his religious beliefs, prompting the trade.

With Gretzky re-writing the record book, the Oilers exploded into the NHL's high-rent district by finishing second to the Islanders in the 1981-82 overall standings. Edmonton's 111 points represented a 37-point improvement from the previous year. Before winning the Stanley Cup, however, the Oilers were to learn a pair of valuable lessons. The initial one involved humility. A devastating first-round playoff upset at the hands of the Los Angeles Kings – whom they had merely out-distanced by 48 points in the Smythe Division standings – squelched any false delusions of grandeur the Edmonton players may have possessed. A well-known newspaper columnist referred to the Oilers as "weak-kneed wimps" – a rather callous vilification of a team that was on the threshold of greatness.

1982 – Drafting 20th in the annual June lottery of amateurs, Edmonton decided to beef up the blueline by selecting Portland Winter Hawks' big defenceman Jim Playfair. Other players available at the time included Pat Flatley (Islanders), Paul Gillis (Quebec), Thomas Sandstrom (Rangers), Richard Kromm (Calgary), and Pat Verbeek (New Jersey).

Prior to the start of the regular season, Sather completed two major transactions. The acquisition, in August, of speedy center Ken Linseman from Hartford further bolstered the club's superior skating efficiency. Linseman had been traded to the Whalers by Philadelphia earlier in the day for defenceman Mark Howe. Edmonton sent veteran rearguard Risto Siltanen to Hartford for Linseman and winger Don Nachbauer. Signed, as a free agent, was defenceman Randy Gregg – a University of Alberta medical graduate who had captained the 1980 Canadian Olympic hockey team at Lake Placid.

With a strong center-ice brigade – featuring Gretzky and Linseman – Sather opted for some added scoring punch on the right side when he dealt Laurie Boschman to Winnipeg for winger Willy Lindstrom late in the season. Annulling their "weak-kneed wimps" label, the Oilers breezed past Winnipeg, Calgary and Chicago *en route* to their first appearance in the Stanley Cup Final – whereupon they learned valuable lesson No. 2: there are few substitutes for experience and impeccable goaltending.

The three-time defending champion Islanders clogged up the neutral zone against the Oilers, thus preventing Edmonton's freewheeling attack from materializing. And veteran netminder Billy Smith put on a clinic – especially in the first two games at Edmonton – staking New York to a four-game sweep and its fourth consecutive title.

1983 – Drafting low, once again, the Oilers selected mammoth defenceman Jeff Beukeboom of the Sault Ste. Marie Greyhounds, 19th overall. John Tucker (Buffalo) and Peter Zezel (Philadelphia) were also available to Edmonton at the time. Requiring an extra bit of toughness up front, Sather swapped center-icemen with Pittsburgh, sending low-scoring Tom Roulston to the Penguins for rugged Kevin McClelland.

With all the pieces finally in place – and the disappointment of previous playoff failures fresh in their minds – the Oilers blazed to their first-ever Stanley Cup championship. After a preliminary-round sweep of the Winnipeg Jets, the Oilers ran into a stubborn Calgary team and battled through seven exhausting matches before subduing the Flames. They barely broke a sweat against Minnesota in the Conference championship – winning four easy games – to gain another berth in the Stanley Cup Final against the Islanders. On a team loaded with prolific scorers, Kevin McClelland – the chap Sather acquired for his brawn – scored a third-period goal at the Nassau Coliseum to give Edmonton a 1-0 victory in the opening game. The Islanders battled back to win the second match in a walk (6-1), but the Oilers had it all their own way for the rest of the series.

In winning three consecutive home games at the Northlands Coliseum, Edmonton outscored New York 19-6 and flaunted – better than ever before – its awesome combination of speed, youth and puck control. Executing Sather's European-born system to perfection, Edmonton's strong, agile skaters had the Islanders going in circles much of the time. When Captain Wayne Gretzky accepted the Stanley Cup from NHL president John Ziegler – and took a jubilant victory lap with his teammates – the master plan had been carried out and accomplished in spectacular fashion.

As the Oilers battled through their first Stanley Cup defense last season, the club's exceptional front-office staff began to receive its richly-deserved credit. "You need a lot of breaks to assemble a championship team these days," said Fraser, somewhat modestly. "I believe I have the best scouting staff in the League and we all work very well together. It also helps to get some breaks like we did with guys like Messier, Anderson, Moog and Kurri. They were all pretty late draft picks and we feel very fortunate for the way they've developed.

"No matter how much you trust your instincts, or what kind of secret information you receive, you've got to be pretty lucky to have four late-round draft picks on your team and playing so well. Those guys are really all bonuses for us. Because of our high placing in the standings, we've been drafting low over the past several years and we'll probably do so for a few seasons to come. So it's comforting to know we've compensated by lucking out on so many late-rounders in our early days."

Due, perhaps, to his arrogant, impassive demeanor, Sather has never been inundated with the plaudits he deserves. Frequently condescending towards unfamiliar members of the media, Sather has a tendency to alienate people who don't understand his disposition. Thus, since the hockey writers select the NHL coach-of-the-year each season, it's no great surprise that Sather hasn't won the honor, even though he's been richly deserving of it several times. "I think a (media) person should have to earn the right to speak with me," he says matter-of-factly. "I have a lot of duties in this organization and I don't have time to sit and chat with someone who doesn't do his homework first. I give my time to the writers I'm familiar with. If that bothers some other people, I can't help it."

A scrappy left-winger who liked the rough going, Slats (as he is called) played for six NHL teams during his 10-year career. He began his playing days in Boston and went on to skate for Pittsburgh, the Rangers, St. Louis, Montreal and Minnesota before finishing his career with Edmonton of the WHA in 1976-77. "Slats was very much the same as a player as he is today," says Les Binkley, Sather's teammate with the Penguins from 1969-71. "He was a tough, arrogant kid who worked really hard in practice and never gave an inch against anyone. He was clever as hell. He knew the game inside and out and his success as a manager and coach really doesn't surprise me." A better-than-average skater, Sather never had a scoring touch. His most productive NHL campaign was in 1973-74 when he scored 15 goals and added 29 assists in 71 games with the Rangers and St. Louis.

While Fraser and his keen scouting staff receive much of the credit for assembling the awesome Oiler machine, Sather has played an invaluable role in nurturing many of his players through their early years as professionals. "We got the players for Glen but he developed them," Fraser says. "He eased them in, lived patiently through their growing periods, and didn't get down on them for making mistakes. A guy like (Paul) Coffey is a classic example. He was very shaky, defensively, in his first two seasons but Glen stuck with him and allowed him to learn from his errors. You can see the results."

Sather must also be praised for the relative harmony that exists within the Oiler dressing room. It isn't easy coaching a team of superstars – in any sport. Remember the New York Yankees of the late 1970s? They won, but they couldn't stand the sight of one another. The Oilers, on the other hand, appear to enjoy being together and that comradery is obvious during practice sessions. The players approach their various drills sincerely, but they also have a heck of a lot of fun – the kind of fun that winning breeds. "We're a pretty loose bunch," says Coffey. "We get serious when we have to, but otherwise we're just like most other kids in their early and mid 20s. We hack around a bit. The coaches deserve a lot of credit for treating us like adults and allowing us to be ourselves. They know we'll respond when the puck is dropped."

Sather is quick to credit his able assistants – Bruce MacGregor, John Muckler and Ted Green – for enabling him to concentrate on his triple role as president, general manager and head coach. "I'm fortunate to be surrounded by good hockey minds," he often says. "It makes my job so much easier." All three had prior NHL experience before joining the Oilers.

MacGregor – Sather's managerial assistant – toiled in the NHL with Detroit and the Rangers between 1960-61 and 1973-74. A strong defensive forward who averaged close to 20 goals per season, MacGregor finished his playing career with the WHA Oilers in 1976. He and Sather were teammates with the Rangers from 1971-73.

Assistant coach Muckler had a brief NHL stint midway through the 1968-69 season, when he relieved Wren Blair as head coach of the Minnesota North Stars. Burdened with a horrible team that year, Muckler compiled a 6-23-6 record in 35 games behind the Minnesota bench. His thorough knowledge of the game – in particular his ability to analyze opponents' strengths and deficiencies – will almost certainly earn Muckler the Oilers' head coaching position when Sather decides to step down and concentrate fully on his managerial responsibilities.

Green and Sather were teammates in Boston from 1966-69. "Terrible Teddy" – as he was known during the "Big, Bad Bruin" days of the late 1960s and early '70s – joined the Oiler coaching staff in 1981-82 after a two-year hiatus from the big leagues. He completed his 18-year playing career with the WHA Winnipeg Jets in 1978-79 and spent the following two seasons coaching intermediate-level hockey in Manitoba. His desire to re-join the Jets in the NHL the following year – as an assistant coach – did not sit well with Winnipeg general manager John Ferguson, a former Montreal Canadien with whom Green had many a bitter battle during his playing days. "I really think there were people who would have liked me to

13

join the (Winnipeg) organization, but Fergie didn't want me," Green recalls. "(Agent) Don Baizley had mentioned to Glen Sather that I was looking for a coaching job and Slats called me that afternoon at a hotel where I was busy cutting meat. I flew to Edmonton the next morning and he hired me. It's been a real great experience working with Glen and John."

Watching the Oilers in action is a treat no other hockey team can provide. To think that fans in Edmonton get to see that club 40 times each season... well, they're privileged to say the least. With talent and savvy at every position, the Oilers do not possess a glaring weakness. It has often been preached – mainly by people stretching to find a flaw in the system – that the Oilers' defensive efficiency in terms of goals-against is perennially inflated. Sather, however, prefers to emphasize the club's wide disparity between goals scored and goals allowed. For instance, in their Stanley Cup season of 1983-84, the Oilers yielded 314 goals for only the 10th-best defensive record in the NHL. But they pumped in a League-record 446 markers – 132 more than they conceded. In 1984-85, the Oilers counted 401 tallies and they reduced their allowance to 298 – a difference of 103 goals. "That's the stat we go by," says Sather. "We have reduced our goals-against total the past three years but we still like to play a wide-open, offensive style which leaves us a bit vulnerable defensively. Thanks to our superior personnel, we're able to do things a little differently than most teams."

Sather's discernible arrogance rubs off on his charges – more so in the way they play than the manner in which they deal with other people. The Oiler players are often referred to as "cocky and egotistical", but many of them are delightful persons to have a chat with. Catch Anderson, Messier or Coffey in a hotel lobby one day and they'll overwhelm you with their charm and humility. Gretzky is the same way, only he's intelligent enough to realize he can't hang around hotel lobbies.

Edmonton's alleged arrogance surfaces as a team when the players don their blue and orange sweaters. To a man, they sincerely believe they can beat any opponent, and that confidence provides the club with a precious intangible.

"When I look at the Edmonton Oilers, I really think they have a similar team to what we had in the early 70s," says Phil Esposito, who led the Boston Bruin scoring machine of that era. "Maybe they skate a little better and they have more overall guys who can score. But, it's the same sort of style. They also have the same confidence we had. I get a big charge when people say the Oilers are cocky and over-confident. I can tell you from first-hand experience that you need your players to react in that fashion if you want to win the Stanley Cup. No team has ever won a championship by questioning its ability."

That edge in quality begins and ends with Gretzky. It is nigh impossible to write or say anything about this incredible athlete that hasn't been written or said a thousand times before. He is simply the most dominant figure in current-day professional sport, and the most innately-talented hockey player who ever lived. The manner in which he perceives the pattern and flow of a hockey game is uncanny and his anticipatory skills defy comprehension. He obviously has certain neurological advantages over the average human being, although these inherent qualities have never been fully explained.

Gretzky's most prominent example of dexterity involves the manner in which he can distort time. He'll break in on goal, pull to his forehand, and hold onto the puck for a split second longer than the anticipated rhythm of the play. As a result, the goalie will almost always commit himself, enabling Gretzky to slide the puck through an opening and into the net. His passing skills are also unparalleled. He can thread a pass through a maze of players and right onto a teammate's stick – usually without looking. If that teammate isn't immediately in position to receive the pass, Gretzky will slow its velocity so that the puck arrives at the same time the player does. And he is equally adept at accomplishing this feat on his forehand and backhand.

Due, perhaps, to his highly advanced playmaking abilities, Gretzky is not considered foremost as a goalscorer – even though he perennially leads the league in that category. While several NHL players shoot the puck harder – the Islanders' Mike Bossy, for one – nobody can spot an opening quicker, or hit it more accurately than Gretzky. Many times, he will release the puck before he appears to be set – distorting time, once again – and will catch the unsuspecting netminder totally off guard. His shot is not overpowering, but if there's an inch left uncovered, Gretzky will find it.

As a result of his slender upper body and his muscular legs, Gretzky has an extremely low center of gravity, and his skating style is therefore slightly awkward. Consequently, he is not the fastest skater in the game and he would probably lose a sprint race – over a distance – to several of his teammates and opponents. Within proximity of the puck, however, nobody is quicker or more dangerous. His anticipation of the play, combined with his amazing ability to swerve suddenly in a different direction, makes him almost impossible to stop. At times, his lateral mobility is so distinct, he appears to be moving sideways.

While the Oilers possess several other players who are considered superstars – Messier, Coffey, Anderson and Kurri, to name a few – they are a different team altogether, without the Great One. Because of his incredible agility, Gretzky rarely exposes himself to a direct hit by an opponent and his injury risk is therefore diminished. As a result, he has missed only seven games in his six-year NHL career – his most severe affliction being a slight shoulder ailment that forced him to sit out six consecutive games in February, 1984. It was something less than a coincidence that the Oilers went to pieces during that stretch, losing five of the games, including a 9-2 thrashing in Washington and an 11-0 debacle in Hartford – the club's most lop-sided defeat ever. The slump only proved that Edmonton relies on Gretzky for more than just his offensive output. His very presence, in the dressing room and on the ice, provides psychological encouragement for the Oilers and subliminal anxiety for his opponents.

Bobby Orr and Phil Esposito had a similar effect when they played for the magnificent Boston Bruin teams of the early 1970s. They were domineering, larger-than-life figures who were hoisted upon an imaginary pedestal by teammates, opponents and the media. Their mere presence was worth a goal or two per game for the Bruins.

With all his innate qualities, you'd think Gretzky would be easy to keep track of on the ice. After all, he isn't exactly an obscure figure. Still, his deception stretches far beyond his puck-handling skills. Fred Shero, who coached the Philadelphia Flyers to Stanley Cup victories in 1974 and '75 – and who is currently a color commentator on New Jersey Devils' radio broadcasts – notices that Gretzky has a tendency to "hide" from his opponents. "Not only is Gretzky the best player in the world *with* the puck, he's also the craftiest *without* it," Shero begins. "A lot of times throughout the course of a game, his opponents won't be able to find him when he's on the ice. In fact, even his teammates lose him occasionally. If they were able to fathom everything he does, he'd score 200 goals a year. His little trick is actually very simple, but he executes it so well all the time. When the opposition brings the puck out of the defensive zone, Gretzky is allowed to come back late. When the play is deep in the Oiler end, he positions himself along the boards – outside the blueline – about five feet behind one of the point-men. When the Oilers gain control of the puck, he suddenly darts towards an opening in the center of the ice and his teammates are instructed to throw the puck up the middle. The result is that he frequently gets breakaway opportunities."

Is there a method of preventing these perplexing tactics? "You bet there is," says the coach. "If Gretzky positions himself behind the left point-man, the right defenceman must forget about the puck, and pull out several feet to keep an eye on him. That may reduce the chances of scoring a goal on a shot from the point, but when Gretzky's on the ice, you have to do things a little differently. I equate his tactics with those used by the Russians. If you want to beat them, you have to be counting to five at all times when you're on the ice. If you only count to four, then somebody has gotten away from you and you're in trouble. It boils down to concentration and awareness and it's the only possible way to beat a team like the Oilers."

Edmonton's prevailing superiority frequently shows up on the scoreboard, in the form of lop-sided victories resulting from several distinctive attributes. For instance, the club's penalty-killing strategy. There is a ridiculously simple reason for Edmonton's proficiency while playing a man short. When Sather sends out Gretzky, Kurri, Coffey and a fourth skater to kill off a penalty, Edmonton has, arguably, the three best hockey players in the world on the ice at the same time. The presence of that trio – and its collective ability – has to at least compensate for the shortage of actual manpower.

Kurri and Coffey have developed into the most dominant players in the game at their respective positions. Kurri's 71 goals in the 1984-85 campaign broke the existing league standard for the highest single-season total by a right-winger in history – 69 – established by the Islanders' Mike Bossy in 1978-79. The fabulous Finn's most prevalent trait surrounds his instinctive ability to spring himself free for a Gretzky pass. He darts quickly towards openings on the ice and he is highly astute at positioning himself on the slot area. Thanks to Gretzky's precision set-ups, Kurri rarely has to squirm free of an opposing defender in front of the net. Merely by keeping his stick blade on the ice, Gretzky can usually afford him a quality scoring opportunity. "He still amazes me with the things he does," says Kurri. "I never dreamed I could score 71 goals in one season. But Wayne made it so much easier for me. I wouldn't be as good a scorer without him."

During his splendid five-year tenure with the Oilers, Kurri has averaged 46 goals a season and assistant coach Ted Green feels he is being modest by attributing his success to Gretzky. "Jari and Wayne are almost at the same level," Green insists. "People have always said that if he plays with Wayne, Jari will only be a goalscorer, but that isn't altogether true. With Wayne and Jari, it's an example of two different athletes from two different parts of the world who just happen to fit hand in glove. Jari is just as important to Wayne's career as Wayne is to Jari's because he has a sixth sense as to where Wayne will be on the ice. That makes it easier for both of them."

Fellow assistant coach John Muckler goes further: "Jari means so much to this hockey club. He has an incredible amount of ability and he complements everybody he plays with, especially Wayne. I think he might have the best one-time shot off a pass of anybody in the game. What is also very important to our club is the fact that Jari is the type of guy who gets along so well with everybody. He may, someday, become the greatest player in the NHL, but he'll still be the same Jari Kurri."

Messier and Anderson don't play the game quite as flamboyantly as Gretzky and Kurri, but their own particular methods are just as effective. Both players are basically power forwards – each possessing excellent speed. While Gretzky and Kurri will dazzle opponents with their intricate passing maneuvers, Messier and Anderson will simply take the shortest route to the net. If that path is clogged by an opponent, so be it. With superior strength and leg speed, both players have been known to ruthlessly bowl over opposition defenders *en route* to the net. It ain't pretty but it works.

Messier's hell-bent-for-leather style prompted Winnipeg Jets' coach Barry Long to insist that "he would run over his own grandmother to get a scoring opportunity." One might doubt the validity of that comment, but until Grandma Messier suits up against Mark, it will never be totally disproven.

In the Oilers' scheme of rapid puck movement, Coffey may be the straw that stirs the drink. The man is a weapon. When he embarks on one of his patented rink-length forays, he appears at times to be hydro-planing – floating on a cushion of air. He is, without a doubt, the most naturally gifted skater in the NHL today, and he consistently provides the Oilers with that "fourth forward" element – so prominent in the European-bred system they employ.

It is quite common, in this era, to compare all attack-oriented defencemen to Bobby Orr – the modern-day architect. Many times, however, this analogy is unjust, and it serves only to burden a young player with added pressure he cannot handle. Jim McKenny, Ian Turnbull, Robert Picard, David Babych and Larry Murphy are just a few of the so-called "next Bobby Orrs" who failed to justify that distinction.

Ironically, Coffey did not merit similar praise when he stepped into the NHL. He most certainly held a "can't miss" tag throughout the scouting fraternity, but his blatant defensive liabilities precluded any lofty comparisons. Five years later, though, Paul Coffey is the prototypical Bobby Orr clone. He has the same combination of speed and grace as had Orr and his shot is just as hard and accurate – particularly from his customary point position. With the presence of Gretzky, it is not often incumbent upon him to take control of a game the way Orr did. Nor can he pivot with the puck like the great former Bruin. Thanks to his exceptional offensive skills, though, Coffey bears the closest resemblance to Orr of any defenceman in the past 10 years. Benefiting from Sather's patience and confidence in his ability, Coffey has modified his defensive shortcomings to the point where he's become one of the NHL's most competent and skilled players at either end of the ice. The Oilers would *not* have won a Stanley Cup without him.

"What amazes me most about the Oilers is they are winning so consistently with 24- and 25-year-old kids," says Ron Caron, Director of Hockey Operations for the St. Louis Blues. "When I was with Montreal and we were winning Stanley Cups in the late 1970s (four in a row), we had players like (Larry) Robinson, (Serge) Savard, (Guy) Lapointe, (Yvan) Corunoyer and (Ken) Dryden. They were all in their late 20s or early 30s and we relied, heavily, on their collective experience. Even the Islanders had older guys like (Bob) Nystrom, (Butch) Goring and (Wayne) Merrick in their Stanley Cup years. But the Oilers have young, talented kids who believe in each other and I guess that makes up for what they lack in experience."

Following the Oiler lead, hockey teams from peewee to pro are incorporating the elements of a persistent, speed-oriented attack. Long gone are the goon-style tactics employed by the Philadelphia Flyers to win their consecutive Stanley Cups in the mid-70s. And thank heaven for that, says the man who guided the Broad Street Bullies to victory. "So many wonderful things have happened to the game over the past 10 years," Fred Shero explains: "Skill is much more important than brawn, nowadays, and the skating has improved immensely. Unlike our era, the so-called goons in the game rarely see much ice time because they can't get close enough to the good players to do any damage. If there's one drawback to the change in philosophy, it's the size of the NHL rinks. The kids are so big and strong these days that the ice surface is too small for them. Arenas like Boston and Buffalo do no justice at all to the exceptional skaters in the league. A guy like (the Sabres') Gil Perreault would have been twice as good if he'd played on a larger rink throughout his career. I think they should widen the ice surfaces by six inches all the way around. That would enable the skilled players to perform at their highest levels. Otherwise, I love what I'm watching nowadays. The goonery is gone."

That sounds like a mighty peculiar comment from a chap whose players were more apt to mug an opponent that skate with the puck. But Shero attributes his Philadelphia approach to the sociological consequences of the early 1970s. "Back then, every team needed physical players to survive," he says. "Toughness seemed to be a sign of the times. Kids were rebelling against something in that era – perhaps, the Vietnam War – and it carried over into sports. It seemed like everyone was upset all the time and they used fighting as a method of venting their emotions. In Philadelphia, all we did was adhere to that pattern. It would never work nowadays."

As a result, Shero insists he never had to encourage his players to drop their gloves. "I coached according to the material I had," he explains. "That's exactly what Glen Sather is doing today. He realizes he has swift, agile players and he adapts his system to their strengths. In Philadelphia, I had a lot of guys who loved to scrap: Schultz, Saleski, Kelly, Dupont... it was their nature to fight. I'm sure they're the same way today. If you insulted them in a restaurant, they'd probably get up and pound you. A guy like Gretzky or Gordie Howe, though, would probably walk away. So, like I said, I adapted to the personnel I had on that team. Thank heavens we had quality players like Clarke, MacLeish and Parent or we never would have won the Stanley Cup."

A long-time admirer of the Russian hockey system, Shero credits the Big Red Machine for inducing the revolutionary aspects of the North American game. "People called me a 'Communist' in 1972 because I said the Russians were going to beat us (Canada) in the summit series," he remembers. "They may not have won, but they opened an awful lot of eyes in this country. For so many years afterwards, we would not admit the Russians had surpassed us and that hockey did not belong solely to Canada anymore. There would have been no shame at all in coming to that conclusion, but we were stubborn. We didn't realize that hockey had become the second most popular sport in the world (behind soccer). Guys like Mickey Mantle and Joe DiMaggio (of baseball fame) are immortal figures in North America, but nobody has ever heard of them in Europe. On the other hand, Wayne Gretzky, Guy Lafleur and Bobby Clarke are household names over there because hockey is played on such a wide international basis. It seemed only natural that better coaching techniques would eventually be developed in other parts of the world."

According to Shero, it took humiliations like the 1979 Challenge Cup Series in New York and the 1981 Canada Cup Tournament to wake us up over here. The Challenge Cup – a best-of-three series between the NHL All-Stars and the Soviet national team at Madison Square Garden – resulted in a North American disaster when the Ruskies romped to an easy 6-0 triumph in the deciding game. Two years later, the situation hit rock bottom when the Soviets toyed with our very best players, Gretzky included, *en route* to an 8-1 decision in the title match of the Canada Cup.

"That was the ultimate kick in the face," Shero insists. "It forced us to admit we had fallen behind in the race for hockey supremacy and, in retrospect, was probably the best thing that ever happened to us. The day we came to grips with that reality was also the day we caught up to the Russians. Over the past four or five years, our coaching methods have changed and we're much more prepared to deal with the Soviet system of puck control. Like they have done since 1972, we now use all three zones on the rink and we make far greater use of the center-ice area. As a result, we've been able to counteract the Russian system and that is the most important factor in our success against them."

The systematic adaptations made by Canadian teams in recent international tournaments have thrown the Russians for a loop. Canada has defeated the Soviets during the last three major events: the Canada Cup; the World Junior Hockey Championships, and – most astonishingly – the 1985 World Hockey Championships in Prague. In each case the Russian strategy has been countered, and when that happens, the Big Red Machine conks out. Shero once again cites sociological contrasts for this reversal. "The Soviets are trained to follow a specific system – not only on the ice, but in everyday life," he explains. "When that system breaks down, they panic. They don't have any methods of adjustment. In our society, we're brought up to think for ourselves and make on-the-spot adjustments, That's where we hold a big advantage over the Russians."

Shero's theory unfolded like magic during the '85 World Championships. The Russians breezed through preliminary play, undefeated, and then suffered an unexpected loss to the Czechoslovaks in the opening game of the medal round. Shocked by this unanticipated turn of events, the Soviets could not re-group in time to subdue a proud, yet inferior, Canadian team two days later.

A similar situation unfolded during the semi-final of the 1984 Canada Cup. Led, primarily, by a strong contingent of Edmonton Oiler skaters, Team Canada attacked the Russian zone in waves of four and five players at a time. Coach Glen Sather prudently decided to match power against power and the Russians – with all their off-ice conditioning – wilted in the late stages of the game. Relentless in its offensive pursuit, Team Canada pelted Soviet netminder Vladimir Myshkin with 41 shots – an exceptionally high permittance by Russian standards –

and tied the game with six minutes remaining in regulation time on a goal by Chicago Black Hawk defenceman Doug Wilson. Twelve minutes into overtime, Coffey executed a brilliant defensive maneuver that will long be remembered, when he lurched forward with impeccable precision to thwart a 2-on-1 break for the Soviets. On Canada's follow-up rush, Coffey's bullet shot deflected into the net off Mike Bossy's stick, eliminating the Russians from the tournament.

In addition to Canada's successful pursuit of the Soviets, a rather pleasant factor has been attained among NHL teams in recent years: parity. In the 1984-85 season, a total of 13 teams finished the regular schedule above the .500 mark in points – the highest number ever. The last-place team – Toronto Maple Leafs – compiled 48 points. In 1980-81, only nine teams reached the .500 level and the bottom-rung club that year – Winnipeg jets – compiled only 32 points.

The handful of teams that were strong when the WHA merger took place in 1979-80 – Montreal, Buffalo, the Islanders, Philadelphia, Boston – are still relatively solid. Since that year, however, improved clubs from Edmonton, Calgary, Winnipeg, Washington and Quebec have joined them in the NHL's upper echelon. The result has been an overall enhancement of quality throughout the league.

"Parity has come mainly through the entry draft," explains Ron Caron. "There is a greater variety of talent to chose from nowadays. We used to scout only 20-year-old junior players in Canada. Now, we look at 18-, 19- and 20-year-old juniors; high school and college players in both Canada and the United States, and the many excellent prospects in Europe. As a result, our scouting staffs are bigger and have more time to watch various players in different parts of the world. This increase in the overall talent pool has unquestionably improved the quality of play in the NHL and has resulted in greater parity among the teams."

Other factors as well have contributed to the rise in quality. The assistant coach, for example – a Fred Shero innovation – has become an integral component of every NHL team. "Back in 1973, I decided it would be beneficial to split up my practices and work with only half the team," Shero recalls. "I hired an assistant (Mike Nykoluk) to work with the other half and it allowed the players to receive more concentrated instruction in their weak areas. I knew, right away, it would soon become the rule rather than the exception."

Since that time, assistant coaching duties have evolved from mere practice responsibilities into a wide range of essential chores. "It's too much for one man to handle these days," says Winnipeg Jets' assistant coach Bill Sutherland. "Players come out of junior at 18 years of age and they have to be taught the simplest little things. One person can no longer be responsible for working with an entire team."

Accompanying the head coach behind the bench during a game situation – or communicating from the press box by radio hook-up – the assistant can (a) watch for favorable faceoff match-ups, (b) interpret the immediate strengths and weaknesses of opponents, (c) help execute line changes, and (d) offer added encouragement to the players. Most teams have two men behind the bench during games. One coach works with the forwards while the other handles the defence.

Technological advances have also played a significant role in the attainment of parity. "Videotape analysis of opposing teams has been a big help in preparing for games," says Quebec Nordiques' general manager Maurice Filion. "Even things like satellite dishes have contributed – especially with the unbalanced schedule in the NHL today. They allow you to see opponents outside of your division more frequently and you are then more familiar with their tendencies when you meet. It takes a lot of hard work in many different areas to produce a good hockey team these days. But we have a lot of hard-working people in this league."

Judging by the current trend, hockey is constantly gaining in popularity and esteem. The result is a sharp, entertaining product that fans in most NHL cities can be proud of.

PORTRAYAL OF A PUGILIST
Hockey's Flip Side

While hockey is quite often described as the "world's fastest sport", it can actually lay claim to a far more unique component than speed. For reasons that have never been adequately justified, hockey remains the only professional sport in which fighting is an acceptable part of the system. It is a pure and simple fact that the National Hockey League's board of governors could eliminate fighting – swiftly and abruptly – by merely adapting to the basic credo of North American sport: one fight and you're gone. Throw a punch in a basketball, football, baseball or soccer game, and you can take the rest of the night off. Do the same thing in a hockey game, and you cool off for five minutes.

While they stop short of admitting it publicly, the NHL owners still believe that fighting is a vital and effective marketing tool – especially in areas relatively new to the game. Arguments often rage on both sides of the fence. Purists claim that fighting damages the essence of hockey – its unique combination of speed and grace. "Joe Fan", on the other hand, insists that a good scrap adds excitement and intensity to the action and it is "Joe Fan" with whom the NHL gurus side. As a result, physical mayhem plays a prominent role in just about every NHL game.

There are currently about a dozen NHL players who are recognized mainly for their bellicose tendencies. Names like Chris Nilan (Montreal), Dave "Tiger" Williams (Los Angeles), Tim Hunter (Calgary), Dave Semenko (Edmonton) and Paul Holmgren (Minnesota) come to mind immediately as players who would rather fight than switch. Several members of this breed do, however, possess the ability to play hockey effectively when they so desire. The guy whose exclusive role it is to stir up commotion and "protect" his fellow mates qualifies as the quintessential hockey bad-man.

The pioneer of this fraternity was Dave Schultz, who purposely terrorized NHL opponents on behalf of the Philadelphia Flyers a decade ago. In writing his recent autobiography – "The Hammer" – Schultz went on and on about how he actually despised his role as an enforcer. But those of us who watched him in action would equate that to Xaviera Hollander claiming she dislikes sex. Throughout his eight-year term in the NHL, Schultz led the League in penalty minutes on four occasions while poking and gouging his way to the top of the all-time career penalty-minutes list (2,294). He has since been surpassed in that category by Tiger Williams – no choirboy himself – but Schultz will always be remembered, above anyone else in recent history, as the prototypical hockey wildman.

Exactly what motivates a person to assume this dubious function is a question that has long been pondered. The usual response centers around a player's profuse lack of talent and the horrifying notion that he will not survive in the big league on the basis of his God-given ability. This theory has been popularized, in recent years, by NHL coaches who see the need for a "team thug". Grab a guy who can't tie his skates properly and send him over the boards when the going gets a little hectic. Especially when opponents are taking liberties with your "important" players. For $100,000 a year, he'll gladly look after his vital mates. For the most part, Schultz played exactly that role throughout his career – never more prominently than during his early days in Philadelphia. Under coach Fred Shero's system of physical and verbal intimidation, Schultz was no less crucial to the club's success than were the splended talents of Bobby Clarke, Bill Barber and netminder-elite Bernie Parent. He was paid to fight – whether he felt like it or not. Any other course of action would have landed him in the minor leagues.

Since his heyday in the mid-70s, others have assumed the "Dave Schultz" assignment. A classic, current-day example involves the short yet stormy NHL tenure of St. Louis Blues' left winger Dwight Schofield. A native of Waltham, Mass., Schofield led the Blues in penalty minutes (184) during the 1984-85 season despite appearing in only 43 games. He also scored one goal and added four assists for five points. At a husky 6'3", 195 pounds, Schofield was the player whom coach Jacques Demers designated as his "team thug". When the situation dictated the need for a physical presence, Demers tossed Schofield into the fray. When a game had to be won, Schofield sat on the bench. The generally mild-mannered Schofield admits it is a role that keeps him in the NHL but he certainly finds it less than rewarding in most cases. As he bluntly states: "Management doesn't think I'm worth a damn as a player, so I have to fight to survive."

Such a confession is a sad but true sign of the times. As he did during his youth, Schofield strongly believes he could make a significant contribution by paying closer attention to the rules. With the likes of Bernie Federko, Doug Wickenheiser, Brian Sutter and Rob Ramage, however, Demers feels his team has enough talent to compete at a high level. Schofield is merely around to keep the other guys out of trouble.

"I think I could be a decent player here if they didn't want me to be a hatchet-man all the time," Schofield says. "They call it 'playing physically', but all it really involves is starting fights or defending your teammates. I admit I take pride in the way I fight because, right now, that's the only reason I'm in the NHL. But I don't enjoy it."

While St. Louis management must assume the onus for Schofield's current role, the 29-year-old winger admits some of his willingness to fight is deep-rooted in his boyhood. "When I was a kid growing up near Boston, I was a pretty slick centerman who scored plenty of goals," he recalls. "My father is the one who changed me into an enforcer. All of my life, my old man made me feel like an idiot because I wasn't an animal like my older brother (Gary). When I was playing Bantam, he was a big, tough defenceman with the New England high-school champions. He was the most dominant player in the State; everyone was scared stiff of him. He could play great defence and he was tougher than nails. On the other hand, I was a smallish forward who stuck to playing hockey, but I think I was as good or better than any other Bantam in the State.

"For some reason, though, my dad was never satisfied with anything I did. One summer, when I was 15 years old, the Welland Sabres (Tier 2 Jr. A) came to New Hampshire to conduct a try-out camp for the local kids. I was psyched to the maximum and I went out and played my best – had a hell of a camp. During a scrimmage, though, a kid checked me and knocked me down – a real hard hit – and I didn't do anything about it. After the game, my dad came up and said: 'Great scrimmage, son, but it meant nothing because you chickened out with that guy.' That was the first in a series of put-downs, but he was my father and I respected his opinion. It definitely changed the way I played the game. With St. Michael's (Jr. B), I had to fight and I did well. With London (Jr. A), I had to fight and I did well. I started lifting weights and I became bigger and stronger. I started my pro career in Kalamazoo of the International League and I tried sticking to hockey. I got to the Central League with Kansas City but they sent me back to the 'I' after two years. It was then (in 1978-79) that I remember saying, 'I have to make it as a tough guy.'"

While admitting it is difficult to keep himself in a suitable frame of mind for his role, Schofield draws motivation from the scary image of losing a fight. "If I don't win a fight, it's like the end of the world for me," he says. "I run around in a constant state of depression for a week – totally bombed out. If I don't fight it doesn't bother me, but I take losing really hard. I guess it's just a pride thing. I would feel the same way if I lost a fight with nobody in the arena as I do in front of 18,000 people. It really eats away at me."

This "pride" has enabled Schofield to remember just about every fight he's had in the NHL. And he doesn't go around picking on midgets, either. "Oh, I've fought 'em all in my time," he says. "Pretty tough customers, too. My first NHL fight was against Paul Holmgren when he played for Philadelphia. I was with Montreal and it was during an exhibition game in 1981 against the Flyers. Robert Picard, my defence partner that night, warned me about Holmgren before the game and I remember being a little scared of the guy. He was a legend back then when it came to fighting and the Canadiens didn't bring me up to lead their powerplay. So, it was pretty safe to say that we'd get into it eventually."

As it turned out, Schofield and Holmgren became acquainted early in the game. "He ran at me on the first shift and knocked me three-quarters of the way over the boards into the penalty box," Schofield recalls. "That got me a little mad. The puck went into the corner and when I turned around, he gave me an elbow in my eye. So I figured I'd better take charge of the situation and I suckered him with a right hand in the side of the head when he came off the boards. It wasn't really a fair thing to do but I wasn't going to let him get the upper hand. He went down to his knees and I could've nailed him again. But I didn't want to take advantage of him while he was down.

"The linesmen moved in and we both went to the ice. He tried to gouge the inside of my mouth and I tried to bite his finger. After being separated, Holmgren was going nuts. He kept screaming 'I'll kill you! I'll kill you!' but he couldn't get at me. I was cool and I think I remember saying, 'Hey, relax Holmgren. You're not gonna hurt anyone.' And he's never bothered me since. I figured the next time we played Philly, he'd get back at me. But nothing happened. The next day in the paper, there was a picture of (referee) Bruce Hood pointing at me to go to the dressing room. I had a wicked shiner from the fight but I felt good that I held my own against one of the toughest guys in the league."

Schofield's first regular-season game in a Canadiens' uniform – at Edmonton – brought him together with Oilers' slugger Dave Semenko. "The Habs called me up for five days in the 1982-83 season and we went out west on a road trip," Schofield remembers. "I guess they figured I didn't know anything about playing hockey because they were scared stiff to put me on the ice in Edmonton until the third period. We were getting cleaned, though, so they sent me out for my first shift late in the game. Before facing off against Semenko, Chris Nilan came over and told me to be ready if something started. For some reason, he figured a fight would ensue. So I expected it.

"About 20 seconds later, I took Semenko out in front of the net and he got up annoyed. Because of his size, he tends to get a little more room than most players and I guess he figured he wasn't going to let some new guy push him around. So he dropped his gloves. I wasn't really anxious to get involved with him. I remember watching him in the warm-up and he looked as big as a house. But I'd rather get killed than wimp out so I said to myself, 'Here I go'. We started shadow boxing and he waved me in towards him, but I didn't go for it. Finally, we went toe-to-toe and I did alright against him. When we separated, all my little French teammates gave me 'high fives' and I remember the crowd didn't boo me on the way to the penalty box. It almost seemed like they wanted Semenko to get beaten."

While admitting he plays the role of an enforcer, Schofield insists he has never been told, flatly, to go out and fight an opponent. Occasionally, though, a subtle hint is passed his way.

"We played in Detroit early last season and Tiger Williams hammered Mark Reeds – one of our smaller guys," he recalls. "He gave Reeds quite a shiner. So, before our next game with Detroit, (coach) Demers came up and said he was starting me on left wing, across from Williams. Well, I didn't have to be a professor to figure that one out. I knew Williams would figure something was up, too, because it's not every game that I start on left wing – or anywhere, for that matter. In the dressing room before the game, I was busy deciding what I was going to do with Williams. My heart was really pounding and my knees were shaking with anticipation. I didn't want to turn around in the face-off circle and sucker him, so I was figuring out how I would handle the situation.

"As we were lining up for the start of the game, I turned to him and said, 'The next time you want to try somebody, don't be messing around with one of our little munchkins.' As the puck was dropped, he got his stick up and started yapping at me. He kept it up until I grabbed it away from him, but we didn't get into it very heavily. I didn't really want to go and I don't think he did, either."

Williams, evidently, was even less aggravated than Schofield thought. "When I got to the penalty box, I heard someone yell, 'Hey Dwight, you seen the strap for my helmet?' I looked over and it was Williams calling me. I said, 'No, sorry', and I laughed. I couldn't believe he was calling me by my first name. If he'd have said, 'Hey, punk', or something, I wouldn't have been surprised. But there he was, talking to me like a buddy after we had almost gotten into a brawl. It was funny. I never heard anything further from Williams until I read an article a few weeks later. He was talking about some of the tough guys in the league and he prefixed my name with an obscenity. He talked about 'that Nilan, and that Wilson and that ***** Schofield.' For some reason, he was mad at me – maybe because I didn't find his chin strap."

Schofield says he never carries a grudge against an opponent off the ice. But there are some players he dislikes more than others. "Dave Brown of Philadelphia is the guy I have the least amount of respect for," Schofield admits. "In fact, I think he's a jerk. A guy like Al Secord (of Chicago) is someone who I look up to because he's tough as hell – probably the toughest guy in the league – and he can also play the game so well. A guy like Brown couldn't put the puck in the ocean from a dock. But he is a tough customer. And he's hard to fight because he's a lefty. Most guys are right-handed and you get used to being punched from one side. With Brown, you think you're moving away from his punch when, in fact, you're moving right into it. So, he's a little tricky.

"We never liked each other in the minors. When he came up with Philly two years ago, we had a pretty wild scrap in St. Louis. (Flyer defenceman) Brad Marsh gave me a cheap shot so I suckered him in the back of the head. Then Brown came over and suckered me. I took care of him pretty good in the fight, though, and he has backed off from me ever since. But I wouldn't be surprised if we get together again in the future."

Neither player carried his feud off the ice, as Schofield discovered the following summer. "We talked to each other at the NHL Slo-Pitch tournament in Niagara Falls and he let me borrow his sweater when we both worked at the Huron Hockey School," Dwight remembers. "What I think of a guy on the ice shouldn't really carry over to other places. But it was different with Semenko. I looked over at him during the Slo-Pitch tourney and he looked back at me. Well, if looks could kill, I'd have been dead on the spot. So it depends on the type of person you're dealing with. If a guy beat me in a fight, I'd hate his guts in the worst way. I guess that's why Semenko was so polite to me."

Schofield explains there are certain times when he finds it almost impossible to psych himself up for a fight. "If someone on the other team takes a cheap shot at one of our players, I'm supposed to go out and fight the guy even though he didn't do anything to *me*," Schofield says. "So, I'm not particularly mad to begin with. I remember another game against Edmonton, this time when I was with St. Louis. I had been sitting on the bench the whole game and I was half asleep. In the third period, Demers suddenly turned to me and said, 'Schoee, get out there and see what's going on'. Semenko had taken a shot at another one of our small guys – Doug Gilmour – and I got the impression he was being a troublemaker. So I skated by him and said, 'What the hell's going on here, Semenko?' He immediately dropped his gloves and we squared off. As I mentioned, I wasn't really in the mood to fight. I think I felt more like going home to bed. But if I'm confronted, I get going in a hurry – probably because I'm so damned afraid of losing a fight. Usually, I have a quick temper but sometimes I have to get mad on purpose. It isn't easy."

Schofield admits his role is essential, but he says there are a lot of drawbacks once you become labelled. "According to the NHL, I'm a fighter and nothing else," he confesses. "Even if I feel I can play the game properly, I'll probably never get the chance because of my reputation. I guarantee you, fighting is not fun. Especially when you're up against the other heavyweights in the league all the time. If you pick on a guy who is 5-foot-nothing, you have everything to lose. Kick the daylights out of him and they call you a chicken. If he touches you, you get laughed off. So it isn't a glamorous role to play."

Despite all this, Schofield realizes he must continue in his duty as an enforcer, regardless of the feedback. "My girlfriend in St. Louis told me all the people who sit with her at the games think I'm a goon," he says. "Sometimes, I'm tempted to tell them to get lost. But you know what? They're right. And I don't like it any more than they do. When it comes to the NHL, though, it's the only chance I have."

HOCKEY'S AVANT-GARDE
The NHL's Top 21 Attractions

In the National Hockey League's efforts to sell its product on both sides of the 49th parallel, the business of individual superstar appeal will ultimately decide the issue. The sport itself need not worry, for it remains among the most challenging and provocative of all spectator presentations.

With revolutionary coaching and body training methods, the modern-day hockey player has grown bigger, stronger and faster. This physiological advancement has affected the NHL in a most positive manner, enabling each team to possess at least one superstar player its fans can identify with. In cities which lag behind financially, the NHL is looking towards its avant-garde to entice spectator awareness and involvement. Beyond that, the ultimate objective is competitive balance – an aspiration that will be decidedly enhanced by the skills these players possess.

Breaking down into divisions, here is a capsule look at the top players on each of the 21 NHL teams through the words of the newspaper writers who watch them on a regular basis:

Norris Division
While this five-team sector had perennially lagged behind the others in terms of quality and presentation, fans can be thankful for several prominent attractions. The large, raucous gatherings which fill Chicago Stadium each night often marvel at the wizardry of Denis Savard, considered by many to be the most exciting skater in the League. Going into his seventh NHL season, Savard has consistently remained among the top ten scorers each year

– a tribute to his exceptional speed and playmaking skills. "He's the most exciting player in the League to watch in a one-on-one situation," says Mike Perricone of the *Chicago Sun-Times*. "He'll put the puck behind his back, through his legs – anywhere at all to confuse an opponent. He's always coming up with new moves. I think the presence of Mr. Gretzky in Edmonton diverts a lot of the attention away from Savard. I mean, when a guy gets over 200 points each year, it's hard to get excited about someone who gets 105. But Denis is right up there in terms of entertainment value."

When all hands are healthy, the forward unit of Savard, Al Secord and Steve Larmer is among the League's most potent. The slick center-iceman had 38 goals and 67 assists in the 1984-85 campaign.

One of the NHL's best-kept secrets has played superb hockey in St. Louis over the past decade. Center Bernie Federko has quietly averaged 87 points per season in his nine-year career, but he'll probably amount to nothing more than a good trivia question one day. "Yeah, Bernie has probably been the most underrated player in the League in the past decade," agrees George Csolak of the *St. Louis Globe-Democrat*. "He isn't a flashy, electrifying player like Denis Savard but he's one of the most clever and smooth puck-handlers in the game. Instead of dancing around with the puck, Bernie likes to slow the game down to his pace and take control of it – sort of like a guard in basketball. The timing and accuracy of his passes have contributed greatly to the goal-scoring success of Brian Sutter – his long-time linemate." A perennially unselfish player, Federko has averaged more than 57 assists per season.

Detroit fans haven't had much to cheer about since Gordie Howe left town, but they continue to show up in great numbers. One of the current-day reasons could be the appeal generated by popular center-iceman Ron Duguay. Dealt to the Red Wings from New York after the 1982-83 season, hockey's resident sex symbol has developed into one of its most consistent performers. Happily married and settled in the Detroit area, Duguay has strung together his two most productive NHL campaigns, including his highest-ever total of 89 points in 1984-85.

"I think Ron definitely had something this city needed in terms of entertainment," says John Castine of the *Detroit Free Press*. "He had a little 'Hollywood' in him, and Detroit has always been recognized as a conservative, blue-collar town. So it was a nice change for the fans. The Detroit people appreciate hard-working players and Ron has earned their respect in the relatively short time he's been a Red Wing. He has a hell-for-leather skating style and he gets himself into position for shots at the net. He also likes a lot of ice time."

One of the NHL's biggest enigmas is Brian Bellows of Minnesota. After two splendid seasons with the North Stars, the second overall draft choice of 1982 fell upon hard times in 1984-85, as his point-scoring output dropped by 21. Among the most talented players in the League, Bellows may have fallen victim to an attitude problem. "Brian was named captain of the North Stars when he was 19, and I'm not sure he was mature enough to handle that role," says Jerry Zgoda of the *Minneapolis Star-Tribune*. "Contrary to what most people believe, he doesn't have a great deal of natural ability. Anything he's accomplished in the past has resulted from hard work and determination. Unfortunately, Minnesota isn't a team conducive to discipline. A handful of players go all out every night, but most of them loaf around a lot. That attitude has rubbed off on Brian and he has to change his outlook before he'll be as good as he was his first two seasons." A strong skater with a quick shot, Bellows has scored 102 goals in his three years as a North Star.

It took 55 years for a Toronto Maple Leaf player finally to crack the 50-goal barrier, and now that winger Rick Vaive has accomplished the feat on three separate occasions, he has become the official reason for the team's numerous problems. It sounds mighty strange, but that's how the Leaf organization operates.

"Management wasn't willing to take public responsibility for the club's awful season last year so the owner (Harold Ballard) and the GM (Gerry McNamara) used Vaive as a scapegoat to absolve themselves," explains Jim O'Leary of the *Toronto Sun*. "There's no way he deserved the shabby treatment he got from the team and the fans – it was really unfortunate to watch. All Rick wants to do is be left alone and play hockey. He's a natural goalscorer with a very powerful slapshot and the Leafs desperately require his production. All the talk about trading him is silly. I can't think of the last Stanley Cup winner that didn't have a 50-goal scorer." After seasons of 54, 51 and 52 goals, Vaive slumped to 35 in 1984-85, as the Leafs slid to the bottom of the overall standings.

Smythe Division
The Edmonton Oilers notwithstanding, this five-team sector had garnered a reputation almost as shabby as the Norris Division. Then, in 1984-85, it suddenly sported three of the NHL's top five teams. Winnipeg and Calgary both closed the gap on Edmonton while Los Angeles emerged as one of the League's most improved clubs.

While Wayne Gretzky gets most of the ink in Edmonton – and deservedly so – he'll be the first one to tell you how critical defenceman Paul Coffey is to the club's success. After winning the Conn Smythe Trophy as top performer in the 1985 playoffs, Gretzky told reporters "In my heart, I wish I could put Paul's name next to mine. He's so important to me and all the things I accomplish." A reasonable facsimile of the great Bobby Orr, Coffey is the most dominant puck-handling rearguard in the game today. "He was actually more dominant than Gretzky over the final two months of the 1984-85 season," says Jim Matheson of the *Edmonton Journal*. "His skating ability is such that he blows by opponents as if they're standing still. Now that he's earned his first Norris Trophy (as the NHL's premier defenceman), I think he'll win it for a few years to come. The voters were hesitant in giving it to an offensive defenceman for a few years and that's not to take anything away from Washington's Rod Langway. But even he said Coffey should have won the award earlier."

The Winnipeg Jets finally came of age in 1984-85, and the club's best-ever season coincided with the emergence of Dale Hawerchuk as the League's second-best center – behind you-know-who. Only Gretzky possesses more innate talent than Hawerchuk, whose rib injury in the 1985 playoffs prevented Winnipeg from challenging Edmonton for the Division crown.

"Being named team captain before the start of the 1984-85 season was the best thing that ever happened to Dale," says *Winnipeg Sun* hockey writer John Bertrand. "For some reason, he didn't even garner an invitation to the 1984 Canada Cup team, and I think that was a great disappointment for him. Being named captain lifted his spirits and enabled him to show the hockey world just how fine a player he really is. Originally, some people felt the captaincy might be too much of a responsibility for Dale. There was a feeling that (veteran defenceman) Tim Watters should have gotten the 'C'. But Dale took the challenge to heart and had an incredible season. When the team needed a lift in the playoff series against Calgary, he came through. Without him against Edmonton, the Jets weren't nearly the same team." Playing on a superb forward unit with Paul MacLean and Brian Mullen, Hawerchuk rocketed to third place in the 1984-85 scoring statistics with 53 goals and 77 assists for 130 points.

Thanks to his nagging back problems, Calgary Flames' defenceman Paul Reinhart may never be able to make full use of his abundant skills. While showing frequent flashes of brilliance, he has been mostly inconsistent throughout his six-year NHL career. "Paul might always be a 'what if?' kind of guy," says Eric Duhatschek of the *Calgary Herald.* "He's always been able to come through with great efforts in the big games, but his overall performance against the rest of the League has not been consistently good. There's no question he came into the NHL with outstanding talent, but his back problems have restricted him in recent years. Still, the Flames can afford to keep him, mainly because of the way he plays against Edmonton. The Flames rarely beat the Oilers, but Paul is always one of the standout performers on the ice. He can still handle the puck pretty neatly." A slick offensive rearguard, Reinhart had his best season, statistically, in 1982-83, when he had 17 goals and 58 assists for 75 points.

Surprising a lot of experts, the Los Angeles Kings improved by 11 wins and 23 points in the 1984-85 Smythe Division standings. While veteran center Marcel Dionne continued racking up the points – he had 126 to finish fourth overall in league scoring – his heir-apparent, Bernie Nicholls, cracked the 100-point barrier for the first time. Nicholls had 46 goals and 54 assists in 1984-85 – good enough for 13th in the scoring race.

"Bernie's finally adjusted to the L.A. scene and he definitely is one of the best offensive players in the League," says *Los Angeles Times* hockey writer Chris Baker. "In his first few years, the bright lights of Hollywood caught him off guard a bit and he had a reputation of being a space cadet. Coming from a small town and all, he wasn't really prepared for the southern California lifestyle. He still drives his baby-blue Corvette with the license plate 'KINGS-9' on the back, and he says 'Hi' to his girlfriend on radio interviews, but he really has matured a great deal on the ice in the past year. He's also a colorful player whom the fans enjoy watching. He used to do a dance when he scored a goal but he cut down on that last year because some of his teammates felt he was becoming too much of a hot-dog. But I think you need that type of attitude in L.A. The hockey team is not only competing against the Lakers and Dodgers, but also against the next James Bond movie. So guys like Bernie are good for the game." An accomplished goalscorer at every level of hockey he's played, Nicholls is also one of the NHL's best face-off men.

Although the Vancouver Canucks have tumbled for miles and miles since their shocking appearance in the 1982 Stanley Cup Finals, they still possess the most prolific goalscorer in team history. Tony Tanti counted 92 goals during his first two and a half seasons in Vancouver and he'll likely become the first Canuck player to hit the 50-goal plateau before too long. He is most dangerous while standing in front of the opposition net with his stick blade on the ice.

"I've never seen a player so skilled at tipping pucks," says Tony Gallagher of the *Vancouver Province*. "He could change the direction of a bullet. I'm sure at least 10 or 15 of his 39 goals in 1984-85 came on deflections. It's uncanny how he does that. Apart from being a natural scorer, he doesn't really possess any unique qualities. He's not a big guy or a real great skater but the total of his skills is such that he can perform well at any level. That's why he always plays standout hockey in international tournaments. He's also a very friendly, easy-going guy – great to deal with from a media stand-point." The Canucks obtained Tanti from Chicago in a 1983 trade for winger Curt Fraser.

Adams Division

This sector produces one of the two hottest rivalries in the NHL each year: the Battle of Quebec. The Montreal Canadiens and Quebec Nordiques have gone tooth and nail in the playoffs during three of the past four springs, and les Nordiques hold a 2-1 edge in series victories. Montreal's spring was that of 1984, when the Habs knocked off Quebec in a bitter six-game division final that included a wild, bench-emptying mêlée at the Forum. Prior to the series, the experts had written off Montreal's Big Bird – Larry Robinson – as just another veteran who had seen the light. Well, they forgot to consider his second pair of wings. Not since the Montreal glory days of the late 1970s, when the team won four consecutive Stanley Cups, had Robinson played such a dominant role. Throwing his weight around and clearing pathways in front of his own net, Robinson resembled the guy who had won two Norris Trophies in the latter part of the decade. He came back in 1984-85 and continued his excellent play right through the regular season.

"He played the '84-85 season like he did the first few years of the dynasty," notes columnist Tim Burke of the *Montreal Gazette*. "I hadn't seen him hit guys like that in a long time. Larry is one of those fellows who has to have his uniform ripped off his back before he'll give up. He was in terrible humor during the year everybody was writing him off. He just wanted to shove it down the throats of people who said he was finished. And basically, he did. In 1984-85, he started going backwards a little bit around mid-February. He was tired and he looked sort of gray-green. He had played in the Canada Cup and his season was two months longer than the other guys', but he bounced back and was his old, effective self in the playoffs. All the players on the team look up to him; he's like everyone's surrogate father." The 1985-86 season will be Robinson's 14th along the Montreal blueline.

One of the opponents he most frequently faces throughout the course of the winter is Nordiques' sniper Michel Goulet. A three-time 50-goal shooter, Goulet is considered by most to be the finest left-winger in the current-day NHL. "Michel has finally developed a consistency to go along with his goalscoring ability," explains Claude Bedard, sports editor of *Journal de Quebec*. "He used to disappear suddenly for several games at a time, but he was prominent throughout the entire 1984-85 season. He had a good Canada Cup tournament and he came into training camp with a healthy attitude. He broke his thumb when he was slashed by Kevin Dineen of Hartford and he missed 11 games. But he came back strong after that. He's also matured a lot off the ice. He used to be very shy and uncooperative with the media, but now he realizes it's part of his job. After his first 50-goal season (1982-83), people started to recognize him around the League and he gained much more confidence in public." Goulet's best season, to date, was in 1983-84 when he was named a first-team NHL all-star with 56 goals and 65 assists for 121 points.

Another member of the old-school gang continues to skate miles each year in Buffalo. Despite his 35 years, Gilbert Perreault remains one of the NHL's most exciting players to watch. The first draft choice in Sabres' history – and the League's top pick in 1970 – Perreault played his 2,000th regular-season game on the opening night of the 1985-86 campaign. His flashy maneuverability has not eluded him along the way.

"I don't think he's slowed down a half step," says Jim Kelley of the *Buffalo News*. "If there's any difference in his play, he has improved defensively since the flashy days of the 'French Connection' (with linemates Rene Robert and Richard Martin). He might not be able to do the things he did back then quite as often any more, but he's just as fast as he's ever been. When he winds up behind the net, he can still bring the crowd to its feet. Heaven only knows how good he might have been had he played in a bigger rink throughout his career. The Memorial Auditorium has one of the smaller ice surfaces in the NHL, and I'm sure it has cut down his abilities to a certain extent. If he had played in a rink like the Northlands Coliseum in Edmonton, with its fast, wide-open ice, he would have been twice as dominant. As it was, he carried the Sabres throughout the mid to latter stages of the 1970s." Perreault and his "French Connection" linemates led the Sabres to a berth in the Stanley Cup Finals in 1974-75, but they lost a six-game series to the Philadelphia Flyers.

Over in Boston, where the Bruins have been known as "pluggers" and "lunch-pailers" over the years, one of the slickest players ever to wear the black and gold has plied his trade with stupendous results. Raymond Bourque was Boston's first choice, 8th overall, in the 1979 amateur draft, and he has since been a first-team NHL all-star on four occasions. Carrying on a tradition of mobile Bruin defencemen that began with Bobby Orr in 1966, Bourque was the runner-up to Paul Coffey in the 1984-85 Norris Trophy balloting. And he is still several good years away from reaching his peak of efficiency.

"I don't think Raymond realizes how good he can actually be," explains *Boston Globe* hockey writer Fran Rosa. "For some reason, he's still a little hesistant when he has the opportunity to take charge of a game. He doesn't pick up the puck and wheel with it often enough, like Coffey does. When he decides to take charge, he can be totally awesome – at both ends of the ice. I remember a playoff game against the Islanders a few years ago, when he had to play left wing because of injuries. He grabbed a hold of the puck on one rush, went the length of the ice, deked Billy Smith to his knees, and backhanded a high shot into the net. It took me right back to Orr in his prime. I think he has to do that more often."

If there is such a thing as the sophomore jinx, it took its toll on Sylvain Turgeon in 1984-85. The crafty left winger – Hartford's first choice, 2nd overall, in the 1983 amateur draft – pulled an abdominal muscle, and it kept him out of 16 games. He finished the year with 31 goals in 64 games, which kept him roughly on the 40-goal pace of his rookie season. If hockey is ever to become a real big-time attraction in Hartford, Turgeon will play a key role.

"He could have that city in the palm of his hand," says Jeff Jacobs of the *Hartford Courant*. "He's young, gifted, handsome, and popular as hell with the teenagers. Although he possesses great talent and goalscoring ability, he has a tendency to be a bit lazy at times. He doesn't often produce in, say, big intra-divisional games in Boston. As a result, he isn't overwhelmingly popular with his teammates. I think a lot of the guys feel Sylvain has the ability to carry the team, but he might not have quite the level of determination required to do that. He's sort of the antithesis of a Dave Hunter (Quebec). I also think he has to find the proper chemistry of linemates. He played with Ron Francis throughout most of his first two years and they just didn't mesh well together."

Patrick Division

The Philadelphia Flyers ended the New York Islanders' long-time domination of this sector in the 1984-85 playoffs by eliminating the four-time Stanley Cup champions in the division final. Young, swift and determined, the well-coached Flyers fought their way to the Stanley Cup title round, before finally coming to rest against Edmonton.

Leading the Flyers up front was a 1980s version of the "Friendly Giant." Oft-injured center Tim Kerr managed to avoid the sick bay long enough to record his second consecutive 50-goal season. When a leg injury forced him to miss the latter portion of the Cup Final, the Flyers had no chance of matching guns with Edmonton. As good as he already is, many Flyer observers believe he could be twice as dominant if he had a mean streak.

"Tim is quite often compared to Phil Esposito in his hey-day," says Angelo Cataldi of the *Philadelphia Inquirer*. "Like Espo, he plants himself in front of the opposition net and the defencemen cannot budge him. But he has to learn to protect his own ground a little more. Because he's so big and strong, opposing players resort to illegal means to try and move him away. And, because he's so mild mannered, he just sits and takes it. The guys are trying to work on getting him to be a little nastier. He's only had two fighting penalties in a three-year period, when he could probably be as tough and feared as anybody in the League. Otherwise, he's a tremendous player. He has a very accurate shot and the strongest wrists in the NHL. When he first turned pro, he wasn't much of a skater and everyone figured he was just some big lug. But he's actually one of the three best-conditioned athletes on the team." With the draft lasting only six rounds in 1979, Kerr was overlooked and he signed with Philadelphia as a free agent in October of that year.

Next to Gretzky, the most prolific scoring machine in recent times has been the Islanders' slick right winger, Mike Bossy. The 29-year-old Montreal native entered the League in 1977-78, and he has never scored fewer than 51 goals in any one season. He holds the NHL record of eight consecutive 50-plus goal seasons and, unlike his team, he doesn't appear to be slowing down at all. Playing without center Bryan Trottier for the first time in his career, Bossy teamed up with Brent Sutter and John Tonelli throughout 1984-85, and he enjoyed another banner year. He scored 58 goals and added 59 assists for 117 points, but the Islanders failed to make it to the Cup Final for the first time in five seasons.

"Mike scores so many darn goals that he doesn't get enough recognition for being such a fine, all-round player," says veteran hockey writer Tim Moriarty of *Newsday*. "Earlier in his career, (coach) Al Arbour wouldn't use him in tight situations at the end of a game and it used to bug him no end. Nowadays, Al isn't afraid to put him on the ice in any circumstance. When he first came into the NHL, Mike *was* pretty much a one-way player, offensively. But it didn't take him long to develop his other talents. He is definitely among the top two or three pure goalscorers of all time. His quick release is unmatched in my books. He kind of reminds me of the way Andy Bathgate played in his prime. He also had a quick release and a hard, accurate shot. With Mike, though, I've never seen a guy who can score goals from the most awkward positions. I've seen him put the puck in the net while falling down, sliding on his bum, and sliding on his belly. He has truly cultivated and developed all of his potential ability over the years."

Bossy zoomed his way into the hearts of all Canadian hockey fans when he deflected Paul Coffey's shot into the net to give Team Canada a 3-2 overtime victory over the Soviet Union in the semifinal of the 1984 Canada Cup tourmament.

Rod Langway's string of two consecutive Norris Trophy seasons came to an end when Coffey grabbed the award in 1984-85, but his young Washington defence-mate, Scott Stevens, could very well become the next Capital rearguard to earn the honor. The 21-year-old Kitchener, Ont. native added a deft offensive touch to his usual strong defensive efforts in '84-85, scoring 21 goals and adding 44 assists for 65 points – all three, career highs.

"(Coach) Bryan Murray put Stevens in front of the net on powerplays and he scored a lot of his goals on rebounds and tip-ins," recalls Rod Beaton, hockey writer for *U.S.A. Today*. "He has tremendous hands, and I don't mean just for fighting. He also refuses to get into a fight with a turkey. He likes fighting the other heavyweights around the League and he's still pretty hot-headed, although he's cooled his act a bit since he turned pro. He's extremely tough to pass at the blueline and he won't let you hang around in front of the net. Rod Langway often says Stevens is passing him as the best defenceman on the team." A tough customer, Stevens has averaged more than 200 penalty minutes per season in his three-year NHL career.

Hockey fans in Manhattan are anxiously awaiting the day when defenceman James Patrick begins to fulfil his enormous potential. The 22-year-old New York Ranger rookie had a tough time during his initial season, but the club's poor overall performance did not lend itself to personal success. A star player at the University of North Dakota, Patrick was selected by the Rangers off the Canadian Olympic Team as the 9th player in the 1981 amateur draft. He practised, but did not play, with the Canadian entry in the 1984 Canada Cup, and wound up performing in 75 games for New York in his rookie campaign.

"Like the entire team, there were occasions when James Patrick appeared confused, lost, and somewhat ambivalent," says *New York Times* hockey writer Kevin Dupont. "The mid-season coaching change (from Herb Brooks to GM Craig Patrick) didn't help sort things out for him either. Every so often, though, you could tell he possessed exceptional hockey intelligence and skills. He's a real 'river skater' with his long, smooth strides and I wouldn't be surprised if he eventually pans out. His development, though, wasn't as full or as quick as the Rangers initially figured."

The two Patrick Division squads that failed to make the playoffs, once again, in 1984-85 do possess, perhaps, the most highly touted pair of youngsters in the NHL. The fifth-place New Jersey Devils are anticipating many years of excellent service from center Kirk Muller, while last-place Pittsburgh has already seen what phenom Mario Lemieux can accomplish.

Chosen second to Lemieux in the 1984 amateur draft, Muller enjoyed a solid, yet unspectacular rookie season with the Devils. He appeared in all 80 regular-season games and compiled 54 points on 17 goals and 37 assists. Without the benefit of a high-scoring winger, he could not make full use of his advanced playmaking skills and he may never fulfil his offensive potential until the Devils acquire a sniper or two.

"I don't think he'll ever be a big goalscorer but he'll certainly set up his share if he gets a suitable linemate," says Walt MacPeek of the *Newark Star-Ledger*. "(Coach) Doug Carpenter brought him along slowly – playing him on left wing with Mel Bridgman. But he looked out of place there, and Carpenter quickly moved him back to his natural, center-ice position. If he continues to mature physically, Kirk will be one of those tough, workaholic centers every team needs to become a winner. He has exceptional stamina and a high level of intensity, even in games that aren't very important in the standings. He's the type of player who will not get a goal or an assist, but you'll still go home and remember seeing him. If they find him a decent winger, I think he'll be a great playmaking center."

Lemieux entered the League in 1984-85 as one of the most coveted rookies ever, and he wasted little time in showing exactly why he was so highly touted. His long reach, superb strength, and uncanny passing skills added up to a 100-point freshman season (43 goals and 57 assists) and he was the run-away winner of the Calder Trophy as top NHL rookie. All of this on a team that finished second-last in the overall standings with just 24 wins and 53 points.

"It was quite a privilege following Mario throughout his rookie season," says Dave Molinari of the *Pittsburgh Press*. "The comparisons people made to Wayne Gretzky seemed like heresy at first, but I can assure you that many of them were worthy and accurate. The guy has so much natural ability. He got 100 points without the benefit of talented linemates, and I think if he was playing with Kurri and Krushelnyski, he'd have been in the 140-150 range. He's the perfect thing for that franchise in so many ways. His cooperation in helping promote the team off the ice resulted in an attendance increase of 3,200 spectators per game, and that helped cut team losses from 5.5 to 2.5 million dollars. I don't think he'll really determine the survival of the franchise because the owner, Ed DeBartolo, can afford to lose money. But he'll definitely be a key factor in the health and well-being of the club if it stays in Pittsburgh."

So, there you have it: 21 splendid athletes whom every general manager in the League would love to have on his side. As hockey continues to advance technically and physiologically, the NHL bumper crop should keep on growing in both quality and quantity.

DEATH THREATS AND FROZEN PEAS
The Life of an NHL Referee

Entering his sixth National Hockey League season in 1985-86, referee Kerry Fraser is by no means a hard-core veteran of the officiating ranks. But he has been around long enough to form an intelligent and objective impression about his rather unique line of duty.

"On the whole, this is a pretty decent way to make a living," he says. "But, you have to be prepared for just about anything – both on and off the ice. In a position of authority, you are often looked upon as the enemy; the antagonist. It's the same thing with a policeman or a judge. If you're thin-skinned, you'll never make it."

While enacting his own position of authority, Kerry Fraser has personally witnessed the numerous trials and tribulations of an NHL referee. Exactly why he opted for this often thankless profession was based, equally, on his love for the game and his inability to play it effectively. Calling himself a "5-foot-7-inch goon", Fraser made it to the Junior A level in his home town of Sarnia, Ont., but he spent much of his playing career in the penalty box. "Being a small guy, I developed 'little-man's syndrome' and I fought all the time in Junior hockey," he recalls. "I never gave an inch against any opponent but I soon learned that this wasn't the correct approach to take. When I got into officiating, I realized you can't solve anything by being a tough guy. If you lose control of your emotions in any situation, you will not function properly. I like to keep everyone, including myself, on an even keel because I find it much less difficult to communicate that way. But sometimes it's easier said than done."

Throughout his five-year stint in the NHL, the 32-year-old Fraser has encountered his share of complexities – some of them bizarre. Having constantly to deal on a neutral basis with players, coaches and fans – all looking back at you as "the enemy" – can become rather taxing after a while. But, as Fraser says, "it goes with the shirt." During the Stanley Cup playoffs last spring, he sat down and re-hashed a number of his more prominent experiences.

Initiation in Denver

"I don't think any referee will ever forget his first NHL game, but I would have to say mine was a little more eventful than most. It was a game between the Colorado Rockies and Minnesota North Stars in Denver (Oct. 17, 1980). That was the year the NHL passed that goofy rule about giving every player on the ice a 10-minute misconduct if he didn't move away from the scene of a fight. So my luck, what happens? Five minutes into the game, an altercation breaks out and the other players on the ice pair off and crowd around the main fight. Nobody gets involved but, according to the rule, I still have to give them all 10-minute misconducts. Well, I'm telling you, I had them in that penalty box four-deep. Naturally, the fans were going crazy and the players were giving it to me from all sides. Walt McKechnie was playing for Colorado and he must have called me a 'stupid rookie' a hundred times that night. Neither the players nor the fans were aware of the new rule and that's why they reacted so bitterly. I made it through the game (a 5-5 tie) and afterwards (linesman) Jim Christinson and I were walking up a ramp outside the arena to catch a cab. A bunch of red-neck fans were lined up, waiting for us to come out, and they began yelling insults at me over and over. It was a little intimidating, I must admit. Glen Sharpley of Minnesota was watching the scene and he turned to us and said 'Don't worry guys, if you need any help, I'll be there.' Jim looked back and said 'Thanks for the offer, Glen, but I've seen you fight before!' All three of us laughed and we got out of there without any trouble."

Gretzky Should be a High-jumper

"The rule book states that only team captains, or designated alternatives, can discuss problems with the referee. But I'll listen to certain players, even if they're not captains. The one guy who stands out in this category is Doug Wilson of Chicago. He is a first-class act –

very polite on the ice – and he never tries to embarrass you in front of the fans. So, if he has something to say, I'll usually give him time. The captain I respect the most is Bob Cainey of Montreal. He's probably the most sarcastic player I've ever dealt with, but I overlook it because of the way he plays the game. He busts a gut every shift and there isn't a harder-working player in the league. He always tries to play mind games with me, but I still admire him a lot. Wayne Gretzky used to give me all kinds of trouble, but he has matured quite a bit since he became the Oilers' captain. Early in my career, he would forever take dives on me in Edmonton – knowing full well he would draw the wrath of the fans. So, I used to get stubborn. Philadelphia was in Edmonton one night and the Flyers were leading 5-2 in the third period. In order to protect the lead, Bobby Clarke and the boys were keeping a close eye on Gretzky and he must have performed three beautiful swan dives in the first ten minutes. Naturally, I didn't call any of them. After the third one, he looked up at me and just shook his head. With about two minutes left in the game, the puck went to the side of the Philly net and the goalie smothered it. Just as I blew the whistle, Gretzky jumped straight up in the air and went crashing to the ice. I couldn't believe it – there was nobody within five feet of the guy. He got up, skated over to me and said 'Kerry, you haven't called a thing all night!' So I looked back at him and said 'Well, Wayne, I'm going to start right now. You just got yourself 10 (minutes).' I'm sure he expected to be penalized because all he said in reply was 'It's about time,' before skating to the dressing room. I'd just had enough of him that night. Wayne's an intense player and he has often admitted he'd like to control his language on the ice a little more. I think he's starting to calm down a bit now that he's captain."

So, You Think I'm a Queer, huh?
"As a referee, you know you're going to get all kinds of heck from fans around the league, and the golden rule in officiating is never to acknowledge anything the spectators say or do. I stuck to that rule flawlessly until the final day of the 1984-85 regular season. It was a Saturday afternoon game in Detroit between the Red Wings and Black Hawks, and the fans there remember me for the time I called two penalty shots in the same game, against Vancouver, during my rookie season. I had just finished working a string of intra-divisional games, which are always difficult near the end of the season because teams are fighting for playoff positions. I was mentally and physically fatigued and not at all in the mood to listen to abuse. As I was walking off at the end of the first period, some guy with glasses leaned over the railing above me and called me a queer. I was in a rotten mood so I stopped and looked back at him – which was my first mistake. I said, 'Come on down here and I'll show you what kind of a queer I am.' I actually challenged the guy, which was very unprofessional of me. But I just had enough that day. People are so brave when they're 15 rows up in the stands. When I got into the dressing room, I was mad as hell at myself. It was such a stupid thing to do. My two linesmen were laughing but I didn't think it was very funny at the time. Early in the second period I was still in a bad mood when a disturbance occurred behind the Chicago bench. Some idiot in the stands threw an object at the bench and the Black Hawk players wanted the police to remove him. I went over there to see what was happening and a big, fat guy sitting behind the bench looked at me and said, 'Why don't you worry about what's happening on the ice?' I looked back at him and said, 'Why don't you shut up?' It was the first time in five years I had ever yelled back at a fan. After the game, a policeman said the guy who called me a queer was a prominent bank manager in Detroit. I thought that was sad."

First and 10 at the Blueline

"I remember doing a game in St. Louis one night when the Rangers scored three shorthanded goals on the same penalty. After the third goal, I went over to the Ranger player who scored and jokingly said, 'St. Louis is going to decline any further penalties against you guys.' It turns out the player went ahead and told a *New York Times* writer what I said and, the next morning, there it was in big headlines: 'FRASER SAID BLUES WOULD DECLINE PENALTIES'. Sometimes, you have to watch what you say and who you talk to."

Shoot Me and I'll Slash You but Good

"I read a story once in which a psychologist said that the average sports fan goes technically insane for a split second every game. He explained the fan actually loses total control and goes over the edge at least once. I did a Rangers/Red Wings game in Detroit a few years ago and the New York players got into an altercation with the spectators. Nick Fotiu led the charge into the stands and four other players followed him. That's always a very scary situation and there isn't much a referee can do to prevent or control it. When the fracas ended, I had to give all the New York players gross misconduct penalties for climbing into the stands and they understood my position. Fotiu was very apologetic afterwards, but he got a three-game suspension from the league. The next time the Rangers were in Detroit, the very same thing nearly happened again with the same fan. Ron Hoggarth did the game and he found out something shocking afterwards. It turned out the guy who Fotiu went after had a .44-calibre pistol on him. It was licensed and everything, so it was legal for him to carry it around. When Nicki found out, he said, 'Well, I guess there's not much my Louisville could have done if he had gotten mad.' Naturally, we all laughed.

Downtown Manhattan at 2 a.m.

"New York City is a real nut-cracker place. Don't let anyone tell you otherwise. Games in Madison Square Garden are among the most difficult to work because of the wackos in the stands. But I once found out that the insanity stretches beyond the rink. I worked a Winnipeg/Rangers game there a few seasons back. It was a totally uneventful game but Winnipeg beat the Rangers, and they weren't supposed to do that. I had a friend from Sarnia with me that night – a big, 300-pound guy – and he had a bad knee. After the game, we went across the street for a few drinks and then headed back to the hotel at around 11.30 p.m. We were both tired, so we hit the sack. At around 2 a.m., the phone rang beside my bed and it jolted me awake. I answered it, and some guy with a gruff New York accent said: 'Mr. Fraser, I was at the game tonight and I'm now in the hotel lobby. You're not going to make it out of this place alive. I'm going to cut your balls off.' Then he hung up. I guess I should've been a little frightened in that situation but I only remember being infuriated that this idiot woke me up in the middle of the night. I immediately called the hotel security and told them I'd just received a death threat. If this joker was really in the lobby, he would have to be near the house phones and I alerted security to check there first. I threw on a pair of shorts and ran to the elevator with my buddy. You had to see this big guy, with his bum knee, going 'kathump, kathump' behind me! When the elevator door opened, I realized I had to make a decision. I didn't know this jerk from Adam and I figured I would never be able to pick him out in a crowded lobby if I waited until morning. On the other hand, I wasn't too enthused about losing my balls. But I figured my chances were better at 2 o'clock than at 8, so I went downstairs. When I got there, security was waiting for me and there was nobody at the house phones. The call had obviously come from outside the hotel and the operator told me she hadn't given out my room number. I was still in a rage when I went back up to the room and called (supervisor of officials) John McCauley. I was so mad that I didn't care I was waking him up at 2:30 in the morning. I asked him what kind of life-insurance policy I had with the league. I told him about the death threat and I said, 'If he gets me in the morning, I want you to know about it.' He told me to not go down to the lobby until morning and he hung up. At 8 a.m., I met McCauley on the elevator and we went downstairs.

"The place was jammed, and John was looking around at everyone like Inspector Clouseau. We hurried out of the place, got into a cab and left. Like I said, you have to be prepared for almost anything in this business."

One Steak, Air Mail
"Of all the characters and practical jokers on our staff, the craziest is (linesman) Willard Norris. He'll pull the wackiest stunts on you and he's also the best at getting even with other guys. Willy might be in Los Angeles and he'll call one of us in New York while we're out of the hotel. He'll order a gigantic room-service dinner to our room – steak, ice cream, chocolate mousse – you name it, and we'll get stuck with a $25 bill. He once did that to Gus Kyle, who was a color commentator on the St. Louis Blues radio broadcasts. He loved to bug him. Gus was in Quebec and Willy was in another city. I did the game in Quebec and Gus called up and gave me hell for Willy's joke. 'I know who it was!' Gus said. He was mad as hell. Another time, Brian Lewis put soap suds in (linesman) Dan McCourt's whistle before a game in Edmonton. The first time Dan had an offside call, a load of bubbles came out of the whistle. Lewis is also notorious for getting into other guys' equipment bags. I was back-up ref at a playoff game in Montreal a few years ago and he got into my bag in the afternoon. He cut all my skate laces, tied my long underwear in knots and then put a padlock on the bag. He also decided to keep the key. I had to do a playoff game in the American League the next day and I didn't have any reason to unpack my bag in Montreal. When I got to the AHL city, I noticed the padlock and I knew right away Lewis had struck. I had to cut the damned thing open. Houdini couldn't have broken that lock. Then I got in and saw my skate laces and underwear and I couldn't help but laugh. If not, I would have cried. But that's Lewis for ya. One of the best pranks I ever pulled happened in the minor leagues. We were in Calgary of the old Western League and one of my linesmen was a British guy. Before the game, I decided to stuff his whistle with toilet paper. I carried an extra whistle out on the ice with me and I told the other linesman he would have to cover for this guy on offsides and icings. Well, the first call the British guy had was an offside and he blew the damned thing till he was red in the face. Finally, it made a faint, little noise. He skated up to us and said 'By Jove, I think my pea is stuck.' Naturally, we had to work hard to keep from keeling over. We were dying inside! A minute later, he had an icing call and almost ruptured himself. This time, the whistle made no sound at all. Finally, we decided to tell him what we did. We showed him the toilet paper and he looked at us and said 'You bawstards!' It was hilarious."

By the very nature of their job, hockey referees invariably compile lengthy lists of uproariously funny stories – many of which they find less than humorous at the time. Ron Wicks often tells of the night Boston coach Harry Sinden jumped on his back in Vancouver as he was leaving the ice. "The next time I did a game with Boston, I made sure to back into the dressing room," Wicks laughs. Then there was the night in Washington, last spring, during the preliminary playoff series between the Capitals and New York Islanders. Mike Gartner came out from behind the net and scored the winning goal at 1:23 of the second overtime period as the Capitals beat New York, 2-1. On the play, however, it appeared as if

Washington's Greg Adams interfered with Islander goalie Billy Smith and the New York players stormed after referee Don Koharski. During the ensuing disturbance, Islander coach Al Arbour nudged his players out of the way and shoved Koharski in anger. After Koharski had safely retreated to the referee's quarters, Arbour came storming by and he tried to kick the dressing room door. But, he missed – badly. "Just as he was about to let fly," recounts an observer, "his back foot slipped and he wound up hoofing a security guard right in the crotch. The poor guy went down like a Coke bottle. It's amazing what people will do when they're angry."

While referees get most of the flack, they occasionally have some company. Veteran NHL linesman Leon Stickle may forever be remembered as the guy who started the New York Islander dynasty of the early 1980s. He missed a blatant offside call in Game 6 of the 1979-80 Islander/Philadelphia Stanley Cup Final series. New York's Duane Sutter scored on the play, and the Islanders went on to win their first of four consecutive Stanley Cups when Bob Nystrom beat Flyers' goalie Pete Peeters in overtime. Stickle remembers every inch of that infamous offside-that-wasn't.

"There was a lot of fighting and hard body-checking in that series and we were keeping an extra close eye on the players who were most likely to get involved," he recalls. "Clarke Gillies raced down the boards with the puck and he cut across the blueline at the Philadelphia end. At the same time (Flyers') Mel Bridgman was coming towards him and I figured they might get into a fight if they collided. So I concentrated on them and briefly took my eye off the puck. When I looked back, it was right along the blueline and Goring had possession. He raced in and passed to Duane Sutter, who scored. As far as I knew, it was a routine play and I went to retrieve the puck from the net. When I turned around, I was encased by four or five Philadelphia players and I immediately knew there was a problem.

"They had their say and the period ended. When I got into the dressing room (supervisors) Frank Udvari and Scotty Morrison came down and told me about the mistake. When I was concentrating on Gillies and Bridgman, the puck came out across the blueline (by about 12 inches) and Goring carried it back in. When I looked back, Goring was already inside the zone. I felt pretty badly afterwards."

Stickle chose a rather prominent moment to make the error. The Cup Final match was televised, nationally, across Canada and the U.S.A., and the fans in Philadelphia did not easily forget him. "I had grown a moustache over the summer and I worked an exhibition game at the Spectrum the following season," Stickle remembers. "When I came out for the start of the game, the fans booed me like crazy and there was a 60-foot sign at one end of the arena. It was a picture of a gigantic moustache and underneath were the words 'WE STILL KNOW WHO YOU ARE!' Somebody brought it down to me after the game and I've kept it ever since."

ARTIFICIAL INSANITY
The Perception of an NHL Goaltender

The essential belief with the general sporting public that hockey goaltenders lack basic human rationale is not altogether true. Mind you, it isn't a pathological fib, either. Ask 10 guys to stand in front of a flying piece of rubber and the one guy who agrees will surely be branded a loon. Due to extenuating circumstances, however, there's more to a netminder's cerebral imbalance than meets the eye.

"First of all, we aren't born crazy," reports Glenn Resch, rather happily. Otherwise known as "Chico", Resch has toiled amidst the NHL wars for the past 12 seasons – the first seven with the New York Islanders, and the last five as a target with the New Jersey Devils (nee Colorado Rockies). "I guess we've always been looked upon as a little flakey or different, but aren't you different when you're uptight and nervous? Sure you are. You become moody and unpredictable during that period of anxiety, but you aren't like that all the time. It's the same with goalies.

"We act a little weird because of the pressures we face every game. It's in the nature of the position. But we don't go home and beat up our children. As human beings, we're the same as everyone else. Normal, in other words. Unfortunately, though, our personalities are judged by the way we act around the rink. It really isn't fair."

Biased or unbiased, this is a picture that has long been painted by intimate observers of the netminding fraternity. The old adage, "You gotta be crazy to be a goalie", will likely hang around for generations to come, no matter how emphatically it is disputed.

"All good netminders have to be a little touched," Resch admits. "I mean, it takes a special kind of guy to go through what we do a hundred times a year. The job itself constantly plays with your emotions. You don't ever want to have a bad game so you're always nervous beforehand. During the game, you're acting out of reflex most of the time. And then, if you do have an off night, it stays with you when you're supposed to be sleeping. So, it's a constant pressure.

"Why do we do it? I don't really know. I guess it's the challenge, combined with the fact that relatively few people can, or want to, play the position. The human ego also comes into the picture. If a goalie does his job well, he receives a lot of special attention – from his teammates, the fans, and the media. Otherwise, I can't really explain, with any great conviction, why a person would choose to stand in front of flying projectiles for a living."

Before an athlete can succeed at this perilous trade, several obstacles must be overcome; the most obvious and critical of which is the fear factor. The prevailing concern over being constantly pelted by hard pieces of vulcanized rubber, combined with the customary fear of failure, drives many prospective goaltenders away from the net at a young age.

"There are definitely two fear factors a goalie must overcome – physical and mental," explains Resch. "Neither one is less crucial than the other. The fear of yielding a bad goal and letting your team down is always on your mind. All the negative attention that goes with it makes a lot of guys flee from the net – usually at a lower level of hockey. Pro players are more understanding in that regard. Very seldom will an NHL forward or defenceman yell at a goalie for letting in a bad goal.

"Kids, on the other hand, will tell it like it is. If you blow it, they'll let you know. A lot of boys at a young age can't handle that kind of pressure and aggravation, so they quit playing goal. If you can get over that mental hump in your early years, you'll be on your way. If not, you aren't cut out for the position."

Being the so-called last line of defence – and the most conspicuous player on the ice – a goalie is the obvious choice to play the role of scapegoat. A competent netminder may let in one "bad" goal out of 10, but he'll often be implicated for six or seven others. This uneducated misconception can become the goalie's worst enemy.

"Being blamed for mistakes that *lead* to goals is probably the most difficult part of the job," admits Toronto Maple Leafs' netminder Tim Bernhardt, who has witnessed his share of blunders. "While sitting on the bench, I've seen fingers pointed at goalies in certain situations where a forward or defenceman is totally to blame. And, I'll usually speak up – say something like, 'Hey, c'mon, that wasn't his fault.' Nobody else understands what a goaltender must go through during the course of a season. But so many people are quick to criticize."

The fear of pain and injury is an element that some goalies overcome naturally. But most young netminders learn the hard way: by absorbing the inevitable bumps and bruises that come with the territory. "It was a gradual progression for me," says Rick Wamsley of the St. Louis Blues. "I started out playing net at an age when my friends really couldn't shoot the puck that well. When they started firing it harder, I had pretty well learned the basics of goaltending and I was accustomed to stopping shots. In other words, I learned at the same pace they did, and that made it much easier.

"If a kid starts playing goal when he's 12 years old, he'll get murdered because the shooters will be way ahead of him. You have to start young and progress through the various stages of athletic development."

Resch believes a young goaltender reaches the ultimate crossroad when he gets nailed in an unprotected area of his body for the first time. "A lot of kids don't have proper equipment when they start playing goal," he says. "If they get hit with a good shot – and it hurts – it'll take a year to heal the subconcious fear of pain. It's like a baseball player who gets beaned in the head. Getting back into that batter's box for the first time is the hardest thing to do. The same thing with driving, again, after you've been involved in an accident."

Adds Rick Wamsley: "Coming right back after being stung with a shot is really the key to playing goal effectively. When you get older and into Bantam hockey, the shooters are bigger and the shots start coming in harder and higher. I remember I didn't have the greatest equipment back then and I used to leave the ice with welts all over my body. There were a few times when I felt like saying, 'See ya later boys, I'm gonna go play volleyball.' But, I got used to it and I stuck it out. Even today, I can't say that playing goal is always fun."

Once a goaltender has mastered the fear factor (if, in reality, it is ever totally mastered), he must then contend with the enduring vexation of watching pucks fly at him day in and day out. Even when they don't hurt, a series of heavy slapshots can tax the nerves.

"It isn't natural to have objects flying at you all the time," explains Resch. "It isn't something that you fear, but it does become awfully intimidating and aggravating after a while. If I threw a cotton ball at your face a hundred times, it wouldn't hurt you, but constantly reacting with your natural human reflexes would make you very nervous. It's like the old Chinese torture test – the one where they drip water on your forehead. You know it won't hurt you, but it'll drive you crazy after a while."

Once goaltenders reach a mature level of play, they often begin to dread practices. Every NHL goalie will tell you he relishes game situations, but loathes practice routines. The actual reason is very simple: he'll face a total of 30-35 shots in a game, as opposed to 150-200 in a practice.

"That's when all those fears build up," Resch admits. "For two hours every day, you become a human target for 20 guys – some of whom are frustrated and angry. If players shoot the puck accurately in practice, it doesn't bother you. Like, I never had a problem with Mike Bossy during my Islander days simply because he usually scored on me. It's the guy who gets five goals a year that you have to worry about. Old 'Cement Hands.' He can't put the puck into the ocean during games so he tries to blow away the goalie in practice.

"I don't like to be a wise guy in those situations, but my usual response is, 'If you can get us 40 goals a year, I'll put up with it.' Otherwise, I shouldn't have to take physical abuse from a guy who scores once every 30 games."

Resch emphasizes that he's been lucky enough to play on "goalie-conscious" teams thus far in his career. Neither his Islander nor his Devil teammates have made a habit of blasting the puck at his head. When it does happen, however, Chico becomes a different person altogether.

"I don't like my goalie personality," he admits. "I'm basically an easy-going guy and I find my mood changes so suddenly during practice. Like, a guy will come down and shoot for the top corner and I'll start screaming. A lot of times, getting mad at him isn't justified because I'm still ticked off over what someone did four or five shots before his. But I take it out on that player. If a young guy, trying to establish himself, takes a rip at you during practice, it's a little more understandable. But when a veteran player does it, you tend to get a bit angry.

"I remember Aaron Broten (of the Devils) coming in on me one day last season. He blasted one off my shoulder and I must have already been mad at somebody, because I just snapped. I started yelling and screaming and I threw my stick and glove over the glass – a real tantrum. I remember all the guys were laughing and I felt embarrassed afterwards. Aaron came up later and apologized, which wasn't really necessary. But it showed he respects me and he didn't mean to get the puck up so high. If the guys in practice don't respect you and start blasting at your head, you have to assert yourself and put an end to it. Ken Dryden always used to say his Montreal teammates were tough on him a lot of the time. If you're a starting goalie, though, the guys will usually have enough common sense not to go after your head. They realize they need the No. 1 netminder and they don't want to throw off his confidence. Now, if you're the back-up goalie... go look for another job!

"We had a Finnish rookie (Hannu Kamppuri) with the Devils last year and the guys just unloaded on him in practice. It really was scary to watch at times. It was nothing personal against Hannu, but you're a heck of a lot more popular and valuable when you're playing well on a team, than when you're not. If the back-up goalie isn't playing, the guys don't seem to care if he gets hurt.

"In general, though, I'd say about 90 percent of hockey players are goalie conscious. I can't think of anyone who consistently drove me crazy over the years. I often tell my teammates not to take it personally if I yell at them. In fact, I tell them to yell back at me and get it out of their system. Then we forget about it."

All goaltenders prepare for games a little differently. Some have the inherent ability to relax and stay calm, while others cannot sit still all day long. Former Chicago and St. Louis netminder Glenn Hall – one of the top five goalies in NHL history – became renowned for his habit of throwing up before every game. Resch often motivates himself by visualizing what might happen that night – good or bad.

"The fear factor comes into play when I prepare for a game," he says. "I worry about the big shooters on the other team and about not being ready to perform my best. I think about the humiliation and embarrassment of having 11 goals scored on me and being pulled from the game. If fear is channeled in the right direction, it can actually work to your advantage by making you aggressive and aware. I also like to keep the situation in its proper perspective. I say a prayer to God before every game just to keep it in focus. I remember (Chicago goalie) Murray Bannerman gave up 11 goals in the first game of the Black Hawks' playoff round against Edmonton last spring. He must have been feeling awful afterwards, which is natural. But I also look at something like that another way. It may sound like a cop-out, but nobody in China gave a hoot that Bannerman allowed 11 goals that night. In the normal realm of matters, it wasn't that important.

"If you're a goalie, that emotional balance has to be there or you'll go off the deep end. The ironic part is you spend a whole day getting yourself emotionally psyched to the hilt and then you have to bring yourself down to a realistic level before the game. It isn't the easiest thing to do."

While goaltending equipment has improved by leaps and bounds over the years, it still cannot protect every inch of the human body. As a result, netminders quite often get stung by shots that inadvertently hit areas not covered by padding.

Several days prior to the 1983 NHL All-Star game, Toronto Maple Leaf center Dan Daoust skated in on Vancouver goalie Richard Brodeur. Daoust's hard, rising shot caught the netminder off guard and he turned his head to the right at the last split second. The puck bounced off the left side of his mask, causing extensive damage to Brodeur's ear, and forcing him to miss the All-Star game. The Leafs' Tim Bernhardt fell victim to a similar shot from Detroit's Darryl Sittler last season. The rising shot caught him flush on the top of the mask and he was knocked silly for a few minutes. In addition, the shot's velocity drove the mask into Bernhardt's forehead, cutting him for several stitches.

"The more I think of it, the more I can't believe how goalies played without masks for so many years," Bernhardt says. "If I hadn't been wearing one, that shot I took from Sittler would have killed me for sure. If I'd lived, my eye and forehead would've been a permanent mess. At the same time, though, I had to realize the incident was a fluke thing and it really didn't bother me afterwards. I've been playing goal for 20 years and I've never been hit like that. I will admit, though, that when I looked in the mirror a couple of days later, I briefly wondered why I chose such a crazy occupation."

In recent years, NHL goalies have taken a hint from their European counterparts by protecting their throat and collarbone areas with plastic flaps extending from the bottom of their masks. Edmonton goalie Grant Fuhr now uses a foam-padded collar protector – similar to, but not as bulky as, those worn by pro football linemen. Mario Gosselin of Quebec did not wear a protective device during the playoffs last spring and he was very fortunate to escape serious injury on two occasions.

In Game 7 of the Adams Division final series against Montreal, Gosselin keeled over when a 50-foot blast from the Habs' Mario Tremblay caught him flush on the left collarbone. Fortunately, he was left with nothing more than a nasty looking welt and he continued playing the game. Les Nordiques edged the Canadiens in overtime and advanced to the Wales Conference championship round against Philadelphia.

Early in Game 3 of that series – at the Spectrum – Flyers' Len Hachborn circled in back of the Quebec net and flipped a pass in front. Both Murray Craven and Joe Patterson took a poke at the puck – Craven scoring, and Patterson accidentally raking Gosselin across the neck with the blade of his stick. Those who witnessed the accident – either live, or on national TV – will recall the frantic, helpless expression on linesman John D'Amico's face as he knelt over a writhing Gosselin in the Nordiques goalcrease. Luckily, once again, the goalie managed to regain his feet and he escaped with just another ugly welt.

While these incidents are frightening, they are still – thankfully – quite rare. Other, less crucial areas of the body are more susceptible to frequent bruising as they are not fully protected by equipment. "I get hit in my elbows and knees an awful lot," says Wamsley, "especially during practice when I'm usually not as sharp as I am during games. When I go down in a crouch position, the area above my knees is exposed and a shot occasionally finds that three- or four-inch unprotected spot. The same with the inside areas of each elbow. If a shot hits you in the 'funny-bone', your whole arm goes numb for a few seconds.

"Even areas that have padding don't necessarily protect you from pain. Believe me, when a goalie catches a 100-mile-per-hour slapshot from somebody like (Chicago's) Doug Wilson or (Calgary's) Al MacInnis, it hurts! You don't really think about it too much because you're caught up in the flow of the game. But you feel it just the same."

Like a quarterback in football, or a pitcher in baseball, a hockey netminder undergoes closer scrutiny than any other player on the team. If a forward or a defenceman fouls up in his checking assignment – thus creating a quality scoring opportunity for the opposing team – it is seldom a mistake that can be readily identified by the average hockey fan. If a goal is scored as a result of that error, it is far more conspicuous, and the netminder usually absorbs the brunt of the spectators' wrath. As a result, goalies often come under severe pressure and criticism.

"Yeah, that's true, but it goes with the territory," Wamsley says. "Sometimes, we get too much credit and other times, too much blame. If you let the criticism get under your skin, you won't last very long in the sport."

Resch admits it takes a concerted effort, at times, to overcome bad vibes from the fans and media. "All goalies question themselves from time to time," he explains. "If you give up a critical goal, or have a bad stretch of games where your confidence is damaged, the sport can lose its appeal completely. You just want to flee from it for good. The media jumps on you, the fans are on your back and even your teammates stay away from you. Those are the times when careers are either made or broken.

"Just when you feel like saying, 'To hell with it!', you have to do exactly the opposite. You have to dive back in head first and start challenging the shooters to beat you. That's why it never hurts to be a little cocky as a goaltender. Tom Barrasso in Buffalo still has a lot to learn, but he's got the right personality for the position. He's confident to the point of being arrogant and some people resent him for that. But his attitude will pull him through some tough situations and will enable him to regain his confidence quickly."

Some goalies maintain their edge and confidence by being aggressive and deceiving. If Islanders' veteran Billy Smith feels threatened, he'll whack an opponent across the leg (arm, back, head etc.) with his stick. If that opponent whacks him back, he'll fall to the ice and flop around like a fish out of water. Should the referee miss the retaliatory infraction, he'll surely turn around in time to see Smith's act. And, more often than not, the opponent will be penalized.

What hockey fan will ever forget Smith's Academy performance during Game 4 of the 1982-83 Stanley Cup final against Edmonton? With New York leading the best-of-seven series 3-0, and the game 3-2, Smith and Edmonton's Glen Anderson jostled in the Islander goalcrease. Smith cross-checked Anderson across the back of his helmet and the Oiler winger responded with a token love tap to the goalie's heavy leg pads. The return "slash" probably lacked sufficient velocity to knock over an empty can of ginger ale, but Smith nonetheless dropped to the ice as if he had just been skewered by a machete.

Referee Andy Van Hellemond, who did not see the exchange, looked over at Smith and figured the goalie was dying, so he gave Anderson a five-minute major for slashing. As soon as the penalty was assessed, Smith popped up like a jack-in-the-box and was ready to resume action. Van Hellemond, realizing he had been taken, approached Smith and read him the Riot Act. But it was too late. With a five-minute disadvantage, the Oilers could not overcome the one-goal deficit. Ken Morrow scored an empty-net marker and the Islanders won their fourth consecutive Stanley Cup.

Adding insult to injury, Smith admitted to having "taken a dive" as he accepted the Conn Smythe Trophy on national television after the game. Flanking him on either side were TV host Dave Hodge and NHL President John Ziegler. "All I can say is there'll be a lot of people in Canada turning over in their beds tonight with me winning this thing," Smith laughed.

Earlier in the series, Smith had hacked both Anderson and Wayne Gretzky as they attempted to swing out from behind the Islander net. Both players went to the ice and drew penalties. Oilers' coach Glen Sather, accompanied by the Edmonton media, attacked Smith with a barrage of verbal indignities the next day – creating a massive controversy. So Battlin' Billy figured he'd try the old trick himself, back home.

"I did the same thing Gretzky did to me to draw five penalties," he told *Hockey Night In Canada* viewers. "When I hit Gretzky in Edmonton, he rolled around and cried like he was dying. So when Anderson hit me tonight, I figured well, hey, I might as well do the same thing. So that's what I did. I threw myself on my back and squirmed. Incidentally, he got five minutes. So all I want to tell the people in Canada and all over the world is: two can play that game!"

Other goaltenders use more subtle means to maintain their fortitude. Resch prefers to take stock of himself after every performance. He weighs the pros and the cons and then decides if he's satisfied with his lot.

"Like life in general, goaltending boils down to more than just statistics," he explains. "You have to decide within yourself if you gave your total best to the situation, or if you caved in. A lot of times, though, we're totally blinded by what we do. It's much easier to kid yourself on a winning team, where you can hide behind a lot of good players. You rarely have to worry about winning or losing a game by yourself.

"A lot of times, a goalie will make 40 saves and lose 3-1. The winning goalie will make three tough stops and everyone will concentrate on his performance. It isn't fair.

"It bothers me to see young kids working their butts off on a lousy team and not getting anything for it. I've seen it happen several times in Colorado and here in New Jersey. They get down on themselves and feel they're losers. They ask themselves why they have to be stuck on such a rotten team. I try to talk to them in those instances and put the whole situation once again back into perspective.

"That's the whole key to lasting in this game. And it's not just one guy. Everybody has to help out. As a goalie, the team has you by a string, and sometimes you don't realize it. I know I can play at a high level only if the situation dictates itself. If the guys in front of me are sloppy, and we lose, I can't get too down on myself. If I blow a game by letting in a bad goal, I have to shrug it off and look towards the next game.

"Consistency in mind and performance is the key. If you can find a happy medium – and you have some talent to begin with – you'll be in this game a long time."

"THE CUP STAYS HERE!"
The Story of Edmonton Oilers' Stanley Cup Defense

In summing up the 1984-85 National Hockey League season, suspense is not a word you would use too frequently. Throughout much of the 80-game regular schedule, the defending Stanley Cup champions Edmonton Oilers, and the Philadelphia Flyers, remained head-and-shoulders above the pack and waged a fairly interesting battle for top spot in the overall standings. When the dust had cleared, April 7th, Philadelphia reigned supreme by a four-point margin (113-109) and was almost unanimously selected to be Edmonton's opponent in the best-of-seven championship round – six weeks down the road.

With one notable exception, the four divisional races were mere afterthoughts as the regular season wound to a conclusion. Edmonton held a 13-point margin over second-place Winnipeg Jets in the Smythe Division, while Philadelphia breezed to a 12-point decision over Washington in the Patrick. St. Louis managed to edge Chicago by three points (86-83) in the futile Norris Division – a battle that was almost as thrilling as the pace lap at the Indianapolis 500. And Montreal earned a three-point final margin over second-place Quebec – and a four point edge over third-place Buffalo – in the hair-raising Adams Division struggle, the only race that captured anyone's fancy on the season's final weekend.

To absolutely no-one's surprise, Edmonton's Wayne Gretzky remained somewhere over the rainbow in the final scoring statistics. His total of 208 points (73 goals and 135 assists) fell four points shy of the NHL regular-season record he set in 1981-82, but was still splendid enough to earn him a 73-point margin over the second-leading scorer, Oiler linemate Jari Kurri. Despite playing on a mediocre hockey club, first-round draft choice Mario Lemieux of Pittsburgh justified his lofty status with a superb rookie performance, based on 43 goals and 57 assists in just 73 games.

Improved teams from Philadelphia, Winnipeg, Los Angeles, Calgary and yes, even Pittsburgh, added to the quality of the NHL's overall product, while a last-place finish by Toronto Maple Leafs in the composite standings had nostalgia buffs (not to mention 3 million embarrassed hockey fans) shaking their heads. In the end, however, justice prevailed, as the two best teams over the 80-game slate met for the Stanley Cup.

Neither Philadelphia nor Edmonton encountered serious turbulence *en route* to the championship round. The Flyers breezed past the New York Rangers in their preliminary round match-up – sweeping the best-of-five series in three consecutive games. In the Patrick Division title round, Philadelphia snapped the New York Islanders' string of five straight Cup Final appearances with a five-game series triumph, and the Flyers fought past the stubborn Quebec Nordiques to win the Wales Conference championship round in six games.

Despite playing well below its level of proficiency, Edmonton rode goalie Grant Fuhr's brilliance to a three-game sweep of Los Angeles in its preliminary set. Without injured superstar Dale Hawerchuk, the much-improved Winnipeg Jets were no match for Edmonton in the Smythe Division title round, and the Oilers swept to a four-game victory. The Oilers then waltzed to an easy 2-0 lead in the Campbell Conference Final against the Black Hawks before dropping a pair of emotional matches in noisy Chicago Stadium. In trouble for the first (and only) time, Edmonton re-grouped and won the following two games by a combined score of 18-7.

So the Stanley Cup round fell into place naturally. It pitted Glen Sather's defending champions – cocky, arrogant *et al* – against Mike Keenan's band of youthful legs and virtual no-names (what is a "Tocchet", or a "Zezel", or a "Craven"?) The Oilers could not manage a single point against the Flyers in three regular-season meetings – losing them all. So this series contained additional incentive on both sides.

Covering the Stanley Cup Final from a media stand-point was an entirely new experience for me. Since 1965 (I was six years old at the time), I distinctly remember watching the old mug make its annual victory lap on television – hoisted high in the air by people like Jean Beliveau, George Armstrong, Johnny Bucyk, Bobby Clarke, Serge Savard and Denis Potvin. For my first *live* Cup presentation – be it at the Philadelphia Spectrum or the Northlands Coliseum – I promised to situate myself in the best possible vantage point (usherettes notwithstanding) when the time arose. It would be something I had waited 26 years to see.

The drive from the Greater Philadelphia International Airport to the Hershey Hotel – in the heart of downtown – took about 25 minutes, but the weather was pleasant and the limo-van driver kept about ten of us entertained with his makeshift tour-guide skills. It was mid-afternoon, May 21st, and the hometown Flyers were set to lock horns with the hated Oilers in Game 1 of the Stanley Cup Final, less than five hours away.

As the van turned north onto Interstate 95, an over-zealous Flyer supporter stood near the street corner, selling Flyer Stanley Cup pennants, small flower bouquets, and soft pretzels (with mustard - they're a Philadelphia institution). Within five minutes, we were approaching the sports complex on our right and the driver decided to unveil his allegiance. As we crawled along Broad St. past The Spectrum, he pointed to the arena and said, "For those who don't already know, there it is – the home of the Stanley Cup champions!" A wise-guy at the back of the van chimed in, "So that's the Northlands Coliseum, huh?", and the driver flashed him a dirty look through the rear-view mirror.

"Hey, listen bud," he said; "them Oilers are gonna be up to their ears in this series. That Gretzky's gonna have Ronny Sutter breathin' all over him and he's gonna wish he stayed home in Edmonton. Just remember – the Flyers beat 'em in all three games this season and they're gonna beat 'em four more times before it's over." Confident he'd made his point, the driver showed us Veterans Stadium (home of the football Eagles and baseball Phillies) and continued along Broad St. to the hotel.

The Hershey is a rather quaint, new establishment at the Broad/Locust St. intersection – about three blocks from City Hall. The NHL had set up its media headquarters on the ballroom level and the Oilers were the guests of honor. A huge sign which read "WELCOME NHL" hung above the reception desk, and all hotel guests received a Hershey chocolate bar with their room keys. On display in the main lobby were six of the League's trophies. Raised on a pedestal stood the Stanley Cup and it was surrounded, rather brilliantly, by the Conn Smythe, William Jennings, Emery Edge, Clarence Campbell, and Prince of Wales trophies. As an NHL security officer maintained close surveillance, hotel guests and fans off the street gazed starry-eyed at Lord Stanley's silverware – perhaps re-living the days, not so long before, when Bobby Clarke had led the Broad Street Bullies in a victory lap around The Spectrum ice surface. Could it happen again? No-one in Philly believed otherwise.

Shortly after 5 p.m., the Oiler players began filtering into the lobby for their bus ride to The Spectrum. Utility role players like Dave Lumley, Billy Carroll and Dave Hunter escaped the scrutiny of autograph-seekers, but Wayne Gretzky, Paul Coffey and Jari Kurri had to be quick to avoid the throng. Gretzky scribbled his name on one piece of paper and made a bee-line for the bus door.

The media gathered upstairs in the ballroom for dinner and dessert – a ritual usually carried out in a lounge at the arena. But the eating area at The Spectrum was already jammed with electronic equipment to accommodate the overflow gathering of writers and radio personnel from coast to coast. The NHL arranged for special buses to transport media members to and from the arena and they began running, intermittently, two hours prior to game time.

The Spectrum is an oval, glass-brick structure, situated at the Broad St./Pattison Ave. intersection – smack dab between Veterans Stadium and John F. Kennedy Memorial Stadium. The latter facility is best known as the home of the annual Army-Navy College football game. Shaped like a huge sardine can, The Spectrum opened in October 1967, when the Flyers joined the NHL as part of the six-team expansion. In late February 1968, heavy winds tore a hole in the arena's roof, rendering the $12 million facility unsafe for further use. Philadelphia mayor Harold J. Tate closed The Spectrum indefinitely, and the club played the balance of its "home" schedule that season at the Quebec City Coliseum.

The arena re-opened for the playoffs and it took the Flyers only seven years to leap-frog the rest of the pack and become the first expansion team to win the Stanley Cup. On the afternoon of May 19th 1974, the Flyers rode a Rick MacLeish goal to a 1-0 Spectrum victory over Bobby Orr, Phil Esposito and the Boston Bruins to win their first of two consecutive Cups. More than 17,000 Philly fanatics went berserk when Flyer captain Bobby Clarke carried the Cup around the littered ice surface that day.

The Flyers won the Cup again in 1975 – this time at Buffalo's Memorial Auditorium – but they failed in two subsequent tries: against Montreal in 1976, and the New York Islanders in 1980. They were loaded for bear as they prepared for their fifth crack at the marbles.

"We know they (the Oilers) have an edge in scoring power and playoff experience. but we gained confidence against them during the regular season," rationalized Flyer captain Dave Poulin. "Very few people outside of Philadelphia are even expecting us to give them a fight, but that's okay. We don't mind being the underdogs. I'm sure we'll acquit ourselves just fine."

Ninety minutes before game time, the dimly-lit Spectrum had already been decorated with signs of all shapes and messages. Strung together around the outer facing of the upper balcony, they urged on the home-towners and whammied the visitors.

"LET'S HAVE A PARADE IN MAY!"
"GOD BLESS AMERICA AND THE FLYERS!"
"SASKATOON'S TOWER OF POWER WILL SEND GRETZKY TO AN EARLY SHOWER. –
GO GET 'EM BROWNIE!"
"WAYNE WHO??"
"CAN THE OILERS!"

When the gates opened, an hour prior to game time, a mob of teeny-boppers decked out in orange and black gathered around the glass at the Flyers' end of the rink, cameras poised. Not unlike the several previous visits I'd made to The Spectrum, the pre-game warm-up was a happening in itself. A party-like atmosphere prevailed, as the Flyers skated to the latest rock'n'roll tracks blaring from overhead speakers. Filling up ten rows around the rink in the Flyer end, young fans danced to the music and cheered their heroes' dazzling puck-handling maneuvers. As *Neutron Dance, The Heat Is On, Born In The USA*, and other contemporary tunes converted The Spectrum into a mini-rock festival, the task at hand – hockey – seemed like an intrusion.

The Flyers have patented a simple pre-game ritual over the years – mainly during home games considered to be of utmost importance. The traditional playing of *The Star-Spangled Banner* is dismissed in favor of *God Bless America*. In the Flyers' first glory run (1973-75), veteran entertainer Kate Smith held the title as the club's official good luck charm. When her stirring rendition of *God Bless America* was piped through The Spectrum, the Flyers almost always won. On extra special occasions – like the deciding game of a playoff series – the Flyer management would fly Smith to Philadelphia and she would perform the song live and in person.

In the 1984-85 campaign, the Flyers introduced a second – and much younger – coming of Kate Smith. Sixteen-year-old Philadelphia high-schooler Renee Veneziale thrilled Spectrum audiences with her dulcet version of *God Bless America* and, coincidentally or not, the Flyers ran up a 19-3-3 record heading into the Cup Final. When she belted out the anthem prior to Game 1 – resplendent in her white Flyers' uniform with the name "RENEE" on the back – she received as boisterous a standing ovation as did the players.

"When the Flyers lose, I feel it's my fault," Renee said before the game. "I'm aware of the Kate Smith thing and I've gotten really superstitious. When I sing and the team wins, I wear all the same clothes to the next game. I also bring my cousin to every game. He's *my* good luck charm."

Luckily for Renee, and the 17,000 plus fans who jammed The Spectrum for Game 1, the Flyers required little in the way of good fortune. They simply dominated the defending-champion Oilers in all facets of the game – staying a step ahead of the speedy Edmonton skaters at every turn. Only Grant Fuhr – in the Oiler net – prevented the match from turning into a landslide in the first period.

Philadelphia out-gunned Edmonton 17-8 in the opening 20 minutes and emerged with a slim 1-0 lead as Ilkka Sinisalo lifted Tim Kerr's rebound over Fuhr at 15:05, with the Oilers playing two men short. Needless to say, bedlam prevailed in The Spectrum. Philadelphia dominated just as thoroughly in the middle frame – out-shooting the Oilers 12-4 – but Fuhr's heroics prevented the Flyers from furthering their advantage. Six minutes into the third frame, however, Oiler winger Jari Kurri made a fatal mistake at his own blueline – losing control of the puck with no teammate behind him. Ron Sutter graciously accepted the *faux pas*, soloed in on Fuhr, and flipped a shot high into the net. Less than three minutes later, Fuhr gloved a harmless shot from Tim Kerr, but his underhand toss to teammate Randy Gregg went astray. Flyer captain Dave Poulin intercepted the puck and centered a perfect feed to Kerr who made it 3-0.

The choppy ice surface at The Spectrum served to slow down the Oiler skaters, enabling the grinding Flyers to keep pace. As a result, Philadelphia was able to clog up the center-ice area – so vital to Edmonton's free-wheeling attack – and dominate, physically, in the corners. Willy Lindstrom ruined Flyer goalie Pelle Lindbergh's shutout bid with Edmonton's only marker of the night – 3:08 from the final buzzer – but Philadelphia scored an empty-net goal and skated off with a convincing 4-1 triumph in what Flyer announcer Gene Hart called "an eye-opener."

The NHL set up a makeshift interview area beneath the stands in the end the Zamboni was situated. The huge media throng scampered quickly to the draped-off section and awaited the arrival of the two coaches. Glen Sather appeared first, stepping onto the raised podium; he was, understandably, in no mood to conduct a lengthy chin-wag with reporters.

"What did you think of the ice condition tonight, Glen?"
"Rubbish."
"What about the officiating?"
"Same as the ice!"

Settling down somewhat, the Oiler coach agreed to analyze the loss.

"We spent the first two periods tonight trying to kill off penalties, and that hurt us a lot," he said. "The Flyers are a superb team and I don't want to take anything away from them. They totally out-worked us in that game. But we didn't play anywhere near the level we're capable of. We skated like we were playing on sand all night – in fact, maybe that was sand out there."

Sather's complaints about the ice surface were dismissed as nonsense by the Flyers. "Ah, that's a lot of hooey," Tim Kerr said. "Both teams had to play on the same ice and we didn't look too shabby out there. We went on and played our game, which is tight checking. We controlled the puck pretty well and were able to dump it into their end and beat them to it. But we know they'll play better hockey Thursday night. So we'll just have to play better as well."

Despite the win, Flyer coach Mike Keenan appeared perturbed in his post-game session with the media. "Uh guys, we've got a team meeting in ten minutes so let's make this quick, okay?" he pronounced upon arrival. In any event, he was gracious enough to repeat every media query over the table microphone.

"The question was, 'How comfortable was I heading into the third period with a one-goal lead?'" he announced. "Well, I was about as comfortable as you can be when you're playing the best offensive team in the history of the NHL with a one-goal lead entering the third period." Simple enough. Flyers' back-up goalie, Bob Froese, came up with the best line of the night after being cut for six stitches by an errant high stick as he sat on the Philadelphia bench in the second period. "I suffered brain damage," Froese said. "I'm on a day-to-day basis."

Wednesday morning: the first day off in the series, and a day of reflection for both teams. Strangely, the NHL scheduled simultaneous practice times for each club, thirty miles apart. The Oilers were booked into The Spectrum at 10 a.m. while the Flyers skated at the Voorhees, N.J. Coliseum, their regular practice facility.

I opted for The Spectrum and, while standing next to the Edmonton bench 15 minutes before the Oiler work-out, I began to sympathize with Glen Sather. The ice *was* a mess. It looked as if someone had dropped a steel demolition ball at center-ice, causing the surface to crack in all directions. In addition, a four-foot cloud of mist rose from ice level, as a result of the 75-degree temperature outside.

"Hey fellas, another day, huh?" said Wayne Gretzky as he passed a herd of reporters on his way to the ice. Oiler back-up goalie, Andy Moog, carried out two practice sweaters – one for Gretzky and the other for himself. He got mixed up, though, and handed Gretzky the bulkier netminder's garment. It was a sight to behold! The Great One had room to swim in his shirt while poor Moog found himself tied up in a veritable straight jacket. It took Gretzky, laughing heartily, five minutes to peel the sweater off of Moog's back. In between beefs about the rotten ice conditions, the Oilers pranced around in good humor and appeared to be more than confident they would avenge the previous night's defeat.

Although he didn't skate, Edmonton defenceman Paul Coffey was gracious enough to emerge from the dressing room in his Oiler bathrobe and hold court with reporters at rink-side. "I thought we played a lazy hockey game last night, from the defense to the forwards," he began. "Only Grant (Fuhr) did his job and he really kept us in the game. Otherwise, we got beaten to the puck all night long. Every time there was a loose puck, two white jerseys got to it first. We can't win playing that way."

After 28 minutes of practice drills, Sather called his players off the ice and waved on the Zamboni. Suspecting a potential sabotage, he followed the driver to the Zamboni exit and asked what temperature the water was. Eventually, the Oilers returned to the ice and completed their practice session. Afterwards, most of the talk centred around the inadequate conditions.

"I have better ice in my back-yard," Gretzky griped on his way to the dressing room. Sather re-appeared ten minutes later and held court with the media in a makeshift television studio next to the Oiler room. "Look, I know they're trying to improve the ice here," he allowed. "I don't really know what the problem is. It just seems neglected for some reason. I guess they tore up the floor four years ago to try and do something about it, but it's pretty rough and bouncy."

Sather then took a poke at the NHL head office for switching puck-manufacturing companies at the end of the 1983-84 season. He said the new pucks were more inclined to bounce and fly over the boards and they tended to lose their shape with repeated use. "They're awful pucks," he snapped. "Sometimes, you'll see a puck like that hit the post and it'll come back warped. We used our own pucks most of the year – those left over from last season. The NHL kept sending us memos saying we weren't supposed to be using them, but we did anyway."

In his final volley of assertiveness, Sather admitted he would have refused to play Game 1 if the plastic water bottles – which Pelle Lindbergh and opposing goaltenders had been using in previous weeks at The Spectrum – had remained attached to the top of each net. Lindbergh often suffered from rapid dehydration and the nearby bottle enabled him to down a swig of water without retreating to the Flyer bench. Looking to remove any opposition edge, Sather put his foot down.

"Maybe we should attach a bucket of chicken to the nets," he cracked. "Or some hamburgers: I mean, what's the difference? If we're going to have water bottles out there, let's have lunch."

"A bottle of wine and some cheese?" a reporter intervened.

"Sure," Sather said. "Cheese and crackers."

Sather first noticed the bottles while watching videotapes of the Flyers' semifinal series against Quebec. Initially, he thought they were cameras. "We made them take the bottles off the nets before the game last night," he said. "I don't disagree with the idea – especially when it's hot like this. But let's not have any surprises when you get to the Stanley Cup Final. If the bottles are going to be there, it has to be discussed with everyone. It wasn't. So I wouldn't give them our approval."

After saying his bit, Sather retreated to the dressing room and sent Gretzky out to the interview area. Draped in a towel, Gretzky had to climb over a wooden table to reach the hot seat, as the room was jammed from wall to wall with reporters and TV cameras. Smiling, he said, "Okay fellas, shoot." The obvious first question involved Gretzky's astonishing inability to record even a single shot on net the previous night. Had that ever happened to him before at any level of hockey?

"Oh, of course it has," he said, matter-of-factly. "The Flyers just played a very strong defensive game and we lacked our usual intensity. But, Jeez, it's only *one* game. Before the series started, everyone was saying we were going to win, and then we lose one game and everyone says we're going to lose. It's a long series. We have to shoot the puck more and stay away from taking stupid penalties. We'll bounce back."

Outside the dressing room, Oiler defenceman Kevin Lowe – the only player on the team who speaks fluent French – was counting his lucky stars in a conversion with a Montreal writer. "Thank heavens Quebec didn't beat Philadelphia in the semifinal," he sighed. "I'd have been doing 35,000 interviews a day!"

Later that night, Gretzky and Oiler scout Garnet (Ace) Bailey sat in the private boxes at Veterans Stadium for the National League baseball game between the Philadelphia Phillies and San Francisco Giants. At one juncture, Gretzky was shown on the big, diamond-vision screen in center-field, drawing a round of derisive remarks from the fans. In the upper deck, along the third-base line, 50 or 60 spectators began a chant of "Let's Go, Flyers!" San Francisco beat the Phillies 6-2 but no one really seemed to care.

Thursday. Game 2 would go later that night but the business day in downtown Philadelphia proceeded as usual. Blind black men with tin containers – sort of real-life Eddie Murphy characters – sauntered along Market Street, soliciting donations. Back at the hotel, referee Kerry Fraser – slated to work Game 2 – had almost totally regained his ability to talk after battling a sudden case of laryngitis. "Don't worry, I'll be okay," he squeaked, before heading up to his room for an afternoon siesta.

All that post-game talk about the Oilers being finished turned out to be just that: talk. Just as the Flyers had dominated all areas of the ice in the series opener, the Oilers roared back and did exactly the same in Game 2. In fact, almost a complete reversal materialized. Edmonton badly outshot Philadelphia and – like Fuhr in Game 1 – Lindbergh's goaltending masterpiece kept the eventual losers within striking distance. Gretzky muzzled his critics by scoring on his first shot of the game (and the series), midway through the opening period. Paul Coffey's blast squirted through Lindbergh's pads and Gretzky skated around behind the net to bang in the loose puck. It was the 50th goal of his NHL playoff career. Tim Kerr pulled the Flyers even at the midway point of the second frame when he rapped in Dave Poulin's centering pass. But that was all Philadelphia could muster, offensively. Less than six minutes later, Oiler forward Kevin McClelland slammed Flyer rearguard Brad Marsh into the boards behind the Philadelphia net, and Mike Krushelnyski centered a perfect pass to Willy Lindstrom for the eventual winner. Dave Hunter added an empty-net goal for good measure with 27 seconds left in the game, and the Oilers evened the series with a nifty 3-1 triumph.

"I had a tough night, Tuesday," said a relieved Gretzky, after the game. "I didn't play a particularly great game and Ron Sutter was all over me. I knew I had to bounce back and get some shots. I was really excited to score the (first-period) goal and give us the lead. Believe me, it made me relax throughout the rest of the hockey game."

Finnish-born winger Esa Tikkanen made his Oiler debut on a forward unit with Gretzky and Jari Kurri. The rookie played an aggressive game and pleased his coach and teammates. "I was very happy with him: it's a great compliment to our scouting staff," Sather said. "I pay those guys a lot of money to find us good prospects and I trust their opinions. So when (chief scout) Barry Fraser told me Tikkanen could play in the NHL, I didn't hesitate in putting him out there." Gretzky was amazed by Tikkanen's composure. "I must have asked him a hundred times before the game if he was nervous and he kept saying 'No'," Gretzky related. "He really fit in well."

The Flyers, meanwhile, didn't dig for excuses after the loss. "We weren't the same as in Game 1," Lindbergh said. "We didn't play with the same aggressiveness. They played better. They were more aggressive." Added rookie forward Peter Zezel: "We know they're the Stanley Cup champions. Tonight they out-skated and out-worked us and deserved to win. We know we'll have to play our hearts out in Edmonton, the same as we did in Game 1." Captain Dave Poulin was full of praise for both teams. "Maybe it was a compliment, in a way, to our team that Edmonton had to adjust so drastically," he said. "The fact they made that adjustment is a compliment to them as well."

Except for the defending champs, Friday was "Travel Day" for everyone involved in the series. The Oilers had left on a charter flight after Game 2, offering a healthy $500 flat rate to media members who wished to join them. The Flyers chartered out early Friday morning, while most NHL employees and media members had connecting flights to Edmonton through either Toronto or Minneapolis. The weather in Edmonton wasn't too inviting late Friday afternoon. In fact, the Air Canada Boeing-767 jetliner I was on emerged from a thick cloud ceiling only seconds before landing. It was also cool: about 15 degrees Celsius – hockey weather, in other words.

The Northlands Coliseum – home of the Oilers – is roughly the same distance from downtown Edmonton as The Spectrum is from the heart of Philadelphia. Located in the north-east section of the city, adjacent to a race-track, Northlands is a round, white-faced structure, almost identical in appearance – both inside and out – to Vancouver's Pacific

Coliseum. Opened in the early 1970s, Northlands provided a home for the Oilers' World Hockey Association forerunner from 1972-79.

The sell-out crowd that jammed the Coliseum for Game 3 got its money's worth right off the bat. A delightful, young sister act from Tacoma, Wash. captivated the audience with the two national anthems. Nine-year-old Kirsten Ostrom and her seven-year-old sister Heather had the crowd gasping with the high-pitched notes they attained. When the two young ladies stepped off the ice, Mr. Gretzky took over.

Within 85 seconds of play, the Great One had Edmonton ahead 2-0. Gretzky decked Pelle Lindbergh to his knees to score the opening goal at 1:10 and he then banged in Paul Coffey's centering pass 15 seconds later. Although the Flyers fought back valiantly all night long, they never quite recovered from Gretzky's sudden outburst. No. 99 notched his third goal of the game later in the opening period and then helped set up Mike Krushelnyski for the Oilers' fourth marker – and a 4-1 lead – in the second frame. Late in that middle period, Gretzky pulled off another one of his dazzling maneuvers that had even the frequent Oiler-watchers gasping. He chased a loose puck deep into the Flyer corner and found himself at too severe an angle to feed linemate Kurri in the slot. Before circling behind the goal, he banked a perfect pass off the side facing of the net and right onto the winger's stick. Kurri – himself astounded – flubbed a weak shot wide of the corner.

The second period also spawned the most controversial moment of the series. While racing after a loose puck behind the Flyer net, Oiler forward Mark Napier took a vicious high-stick in the mouth from Philadelphia defenceman Ed Hospodar. Bleeding profusely – and minus three teeth – Napier was assisted off the ice. The flagrant infraction somehow managed to escape the notice of referee Brian Lewis and the Flyers luckily avoided what should have been a five-minute major penalty. The incident would precipitate a series of warnings from the angry Oiler camp later on.

With a seemingly-comfortable three-goal cushion, the Oilers went for a snooze and the determined Flyers sent a scare through the Coliseum crowd by scoring two unanswered goals in the final twenty minutes. Philadelphia's third tally was a cheap one as Brian Propp's feeble backhand attempt from a sharp angle squirted through Grant Fuhr's pads with 5.34 remaining in regulation time. Despite registering only six shots on goal in the final 40 minutes, Edmonton hung on to edge the Flyers 4-3, and grab a 2-1 lead in the series.

The post-game interview area at Northlands was situated underneath the stands – between the two dressing rooms – and amidst all the TV control trucks. With three national networks – CTV and CBC in Canada, and USA cable in the States – providing live television feeds, the south-side catacombs were crammed full of communications equipment. Dressed in full uniform, but wearing sneakers instead of his skates, Gretzky arrived first at the interview area and had a difficult time wiping a glorious smile off his face.

"I was pretty high at the beginning of the game tonight and I got an extra lift when we scored early," he told the overflow throng of reporters. "You get a reputation for scoring goals and assists and when you don't (i.e. Game 1), it get's frustrating. Overall, I think I played a pretty strong hockey game. With all our 4-on-4's tonight, there was a lot of open ice to work with. If we had beared down a little more on some of our 2-on-1's, we could have made the score 5 or 6 to 1 and possibly put the game out of reach for the Flyers.

"But they don't quit. No lead is really safe against them. Hard work is a trademark of theirs, and we're going to have to work harder on Tuesday than we did tonight."

Sather joined Gretzky at the table and revealed mixed emotions about the victory. "What can you say about Wayne?" he began. "He's a great hockey player who is very self-motivated and that's what makes him so good. Tonight was his best performance in this series. He was outstanding. But, overall, I wasn't too happy with the way we played in the third period. It was a little hairy at the end there. For some reason we started to retreat a little and we got cute around the net and gave up a few goals. Philadelphia is too good a team to let down against and I felt we were lucky to come out with that victory."

After all the technical stuff had been discussed, the media got down to some serious talk about the Napier/Hospodar incident. Needless to say, Sather was none too impressed by the episode, or the manner in which it was handled. "Obviously, the referee was out to lunch on the play," he said. "He couldn't see that infraction when everybody in the building saw it, yet he called all those tic-tac-toe minor penalties in front of the benches. You figure it out."

Later on, in the Oiler dressing room, Sather issued an even stronger statement. "If they don't do something about him (Hospodar), I'll do something myself. We have people here who can take care of him." Napier, who had the remaining chips of three teeth extracted by the Oilers' team dentist, was less hostile, but just as surprised. "I thought he'd get a penalty for sure, but I guess Bryan (Lewis) didn't see it," Napier said, pausing several times to spit out blood. "I guess I've got to grow a couple of inches. That way, he would have hit me in the chest."

Dave Semenko, the Oilers' resident hit-man, was asked if Hospodar was getting under his skin. "Yes he is," said Semenko, who drew 14 minutes in penalties trying to get at the Flyer defenceman later in the game. "I can't believe he (Lewis) missed that call. If Hospodar had hit him clean, it would've been another thing. But that was a pretty cheap shot he gave Napier." For his part, Hospodar dressed quickly and departed the Coliseum without commenting on the incident.

Both teams practised at Northlands Coliseum Sunday morning and the talk centered around two controversial subjects. In one corner, the Napier/Hospodar war of words continued, while in the other, Flyer coach Mike Keenan all but implicated the Oilers for inducing the 4-on-4 manpower situations they enjoy so much. First, to the Napier incident.

Despite a full night's sleep, Sather hadn't yet cooled his feelings towards Hospodar. "If the League doesn't do something about this guy, we're going to get two boxes for him – one for his head, and the other for his body," said the Oiler coach. Semenko, meanwhile, held court in another corner of the dressing room. While sipping on a cup of GatorAide, he answered questions in a calm, yet forthright manner.

"Did you see the replay of the incident, Dave?" asked a reporter.
"No I didn't," he replied. "Watching it live was bad enough. If I see a replay of it, I might go over to the hotel right now and beat the hell out of him!"
"Are you guys going to be after him in the next game?"
"Well, I wouldn't say he's got a price on his head, but he'd better watch who he goes around

hitting. We're not going to go out just to get even and forget about our main task, which is winning the hockey game."

Across the floor from Semenko, Napier looked like a guy who had been high-sticked in the choppers. Three front teeth were missing on the right side while the three on the left had been capped. He also had a nasty gash on his lower right lip. Still, he was in a rather pensive mood.

"I guess things like this are part of the game," he said. "He's a hard-nosed guy and he might have just been trying to protect himself. I don't know if he did it deliberately or not, but I sure hope he didn't. Our No. 1 priority is still to win the Stanley Cup, though. I think we got the message across (to Hospodar). 'Sammy' (Semenko) talked to him and we were told between periods, 'Let's win the game. If something happens, it happens.' But if it was deliberate, something should be done."

Hospodar, meanwhile, ended his own brief silence on the subject and decided to plead the 'Fifth'. "What happened to him? I thought he ran into the boards," Hospodar said with mock integrity. "I guess he's okay. How come he came back at the end of the game? The Oilers are paying a lot of attention to me. When you play the body like I do, people get distracted and upset."

Over in the Flyer camp, coach Mike Keenan was intimating that the Oilers had suckered referee Brian Lewis into creating four-on-four situations. Gretzky had scored all three of his first-period goals the night before, while both teams were skating one man short. With more room on the ice to flaunt their skills, Keenan felt it was becoming an Oiler strategy to produce four-on-four situations. Kevin Lowe's comment about "no one in the League having a four-on-four like us" added to his suspicion. He definitely smelled something fishy.

"I guess we'd like an interpretation on how the refs are going to call it," Keenan told reporters. "It's extremely difficult (for us) to play that way and it's very convenient for the Oilers. I might try the same trick if I had four or five of the best players in the world. But I don't know that all those minor penalties are necessary in the first place. It might be a little bit of over-reaction on the officials' part. It's very convenient to throw two guys off together instead of dealing with the problem. The tactics employed (by the Oilers) in this series are such that the refs should be aware of it."

Naturally, Keenan's accusation was ridiculed by the Oilers. "What's he saying – that we intentionally get a penalty on, say, a powerplay to get a four-on-four?" Sather asked, innocently. "I guess it's flattering if he thinks we can manipulate the referees into calling coincidental penalties. Speaking from experience, I've never been able to get the refs to do anything I want them to." Kevin Lowe was a little more philosophical. "Intentionally to get a couple of guys always going off is impossible," he said. "I guess it could be done a few times, but unless they're holding meetings and not letting me in on it, that's not in our game plan."

Keenan's comment to reporters, that "you guys are blowing the Hospodar incident way out of proportion", further perplexed Sather. "Ha, that's a hot one," said the Oiler coach. "If you look at the tapes, I'll show you one of the classic crosschecks. It's an attempt to injure somebody. Stick infractions that occur in the NHL are generally unintentional, but to say Hospodar's was an accident may be stretching a point."

Much of the afternoon that day was spent at John Ducey Park – baseball home of the Pacific Coast League Edmonton Trappers. The NHL employees decided to risk utter humiliation by challenging the media to a softball game and, as expected, too many players showed up. So the media guys split up into Canadian and American teams and had it out themselves. The stars of the game? Well, there weren't any. In fact, the most competent person of all might have been NHL information director John (Andy van) Halligan, who umpired with impeccable form.

Deciding to keep his players functioning on Eastern Standard Time, Keenan had the Flyers on the Northlands Coliseum ice at the ungodly hour of 8:30 a.m., Monday morning. Considering it was 10:30 a.m. back home, the players should have been loaded for bear. Instead, they looked rather bed-ridden. And they were in foul moods.

During a five-on-nothing drill (real fair, eh?), Ilkka Sinisalo zipped a quick shot through Pelle Lindbergh's pads and the goalie responded with a resounding stream of obscenities that echoed through the empty arena. After a lethargic 45-minute session, Keenan saw the light and sent his fellows to the showers.

Outside the dressing rooms came the enthralling news that *Winnipeg Sun* hockey writer John Bertrand had won the official media pool for "first sighting of John Ziegler." Despite the clamouring of reporters, Bertrand was not available to reveal exactly where he noticed the NHL prexy.

The gala events of the week took place in the afternoon with the Stanley Cup luncheon, followed by President Ziegler's annual state-of-the-union press conference. The luncheon was held at the magnificent Edmonton Convention Centre, and a gathering of more than 2,000 turned out to gulp down a hearty meal of steak and potatoes, and to witness several trophy presentations.

Announcers Dan Kelly of CTV and Don Wittman of CBC emceed the formal part of the luncheon and they stumbled through a 'Frick & Frack' routine that had the audience groaning. After the meal, four awards were presented – two of them to Gretzky, who sat at the head table with Sather. Upon making his acceptance speech for the Jennings Trophy (which he won with partner Tom Barrasso), Buffalo Sabres' goalie Bob Sauve broke up the audience with the best line of the day. "With hockey being a team game, I would like to split the $500 prize with all of my teammates," he began, solemnly, "but I realize all the shares would be too small. So I've decided to fix the problem and keep it all for myself."

Immediately following the luncheon, media members gathered in an adjacent salon for Ziegler's conference. For almost three hours, the writers and broadcasters grilled the President on topics that varied from the League's collective bargaining agreement to the possibility of a future NHL/Soviet Union exhibition series.

Edmonton fans entering the Northlands Coliseum for Game 4, Tuesday night, were handed orange and black "FLYer-SWATTERS" – miniature versions of the conventional household device. Twelve minutes into the game, they were wishing they could use them. Skating circles around the stumbling Oilers, the Flyers jumped out to a 3-1 lead – which could have easily been 4-1 had Grant Fuhr not stopped Ron Sutter on a penalty shot. At no previous time throughout the series had the Oilers appeared as disorganized or frustrated.

But defending champions in any sport usually possess means by which to overcome adversity and the Oilers, as it turned out, were no different on this night. Exploiting the cardinal defensive sin of permitting goals in the early or late stages of a period, Edmonton got markers from Charlie Huddy (18:23 of the 1st) and Glenn Anderson (0:21 of the 2nd), to climb back into a 3-3 deadlock. Then they turned loose their primary fly-swatter – Gretzky – who potted the winning and insurance tallies in a 5-3 Oiler triumph.

Dispelling Keenan's earlier theory about preferring four-on-four situations, the Oilers stuck to their conventional powerplay and recorded four extra-man goals. Included among them was Gretzky's first score – the eventual winner – at 12:53 of the middle frame. He snapped a 15-foot backhand drive past Lindbergh, who would leave the game – suffering from dehydration – at the end of the period. Gretzky then converted a nifty backhand set-up from Mark Messier early in the third, for the Oilers' insurance marker – also on the powerplay. Despite the early scare, Edmonton called upon its abundant character to place the Flyers on the brink of elimination with a 3-1 series lead.

All smiles once again, Gretzky arrived first at the post-game interview area – this time wearing a blue Oilers' sweat-suit. It was another grandiose performance by the world's greatest hockey player, who confessed to both elation and relief. "We knew Philly would come out hard, and they sure did," he told the media throng. "It probably should have been 4-1 or 5-1 in the first period, but Grant (Fuhr) made that penalty shot save and Peter Zezel made a great move and hit the post. We really struggled, and Grant definitely held us in the game."

Gretzky insisted that Glenn Anderson's goal, 21 seconds into the second period, was the turning point in the game. "It tied the score (3-3) and was a big emotional boost for our club," he said. "When things don't go right for us, someone usually comes along and gives us a lift. That's what makes us a great team. Tonight was the most important game of the series. If we had lost, it would've been tied 2-2, and nobody really wants to go back to Philadelphia. Now, we can win the Stanley Cup at home and that was our goal at the beginning of the series.

"Since Game 1, I've been very satisfied with my own play. I've had some great satisfaction in scoring some key goals but our overall team objective is still to win the Stanley Cup." After nearly 20 minutes of questioning, Sather arrived on the scene and said, "Okay Gretz, hit the road. I'll give you a break." The Oiler coach then began to sing the praises of his phenomenal team captain. "Wayne has been the most dominant player on the ice the past two games," Sather said. "When we've needed a big goal, he's come through and I've never seen him play any better. It's amazing people haven't mentioned him that much in this series. I guess we're so used to watching him perform, we become a little complacent."

In the Philadelphia dressing room, Flyer defenceman Mark Howe expressed disappointment in the club's penalty killing proficiency. "The difference in the game was the powerplay," he said. "For three games, we were able to kill off our penalties, but tonight we faltered badly. The Oilers scored some good goals but they also got a few lucky bounces."

Keenan explained why he removed Lindbergh from the net for five seconds in the middle period, and then for good to begin the third frame. "I took him out the first time because he needed a drink of water," the coach recalled. "He was becoming dehydrated again. It's almost June, and with the temperature outside and all that equipment on, a goalie sweats more than any other player. Pelle was beginning to feel the effects of the heat. I felt he was tiring because of the dehydration. He needed to be rested. I think this is a good case for having water bottles on top of the net, especially if you go this long in the playoffs. I can't see why a guy playing 60 minutes shouldn't be able to take a drink. I'm not talking excuses here; I'm talking the health factor." Added a disgusted Lindbergh: "I need water; I have to drink. If I can't have a water bottle on top of the net, I have to leave the game. I'm dehydrated, so it's best I get out and give Bobby (Froese) a chance. At least he's fresh."

With his club up against the ropes, Keenan did not lose sight of his game plan in Edmonton. "Our objective coming out here was to win one game out of three and then take the final two back home," he explained. "Whether we win the first or the last of the three makes no difference to us."

The two Edmonton papers summed up the Oilers' situation with large, front-page headlines on Wednesday morning. "JUST ONE MORE!" said the *Sun.* "OILERS ONE WIN AWAY FROM RETAINING THE CUP", added the *Journal.*

At practice, both teams assumed a calm, philosophical approach to Game 5. "We definitely want to win the Cup here," said Oiler defenceman Lee Fogolin. "Yet, as anxious as we are, we still have to follow our game plan and not over-react. But, I'd be more worried if it was our first one. Everyone knows what it'll take."

Added Kevin Lowe: "I think we're more composed this year. Sure, there's excitement beyond belief, but we're more businesslike. We want this one because people could always say the first one was a fluke; that the Islanders were hurting and were tired. You win two in a row and it's no fluke."

Speaking about *his* players, Keenan felt they were all gaining invaluable experience so early in their pro hockey careers. "Most of them are in a position of testing themselves against a certain level of ability they haven't faced before," he explained. "It takes courage to take those steps, but they have to go through with it. It's so important to the natural progression of the organization."

The *Edmonton Sun* greeted its Thursday morning readers with a phone-in poll to obtain public sentiment on who should win the Conn Smythe Trophy. Columnist Terry Jones narrowed the field to three Oilers – Gretzky, Coffey and Fuhr – and invited readers to cast their own votes throughout the day. With all three players enacting crucial roles in Edmonton's Stanley Cup drive, the 1985 vote was shaping up to be the closest in the history of the award, presented annually to the most outstanding performer in the playoffs.

While a quiet air of confidence prevailed throughout the city, most Oilers noticed a moderation in the overall level of enthusiasm and drama from the previous year. "I think everyone is still excited, but last year was pretty incredible," said Kevin Lowe, "It went back to the city's background – that even having an NHL team was a huge achievement and that to win the Cup in six years was... well, beyond belief. We were kind of like school-kids. We were giddy. It's like getting your first car – you can't think of a better feeling. Last year at this time, you could feel the tension everywhere. Wherever you went, there was a constant reminder of what was going on. This year, it's a little different. It's like growing older and getting a bigger car. It's great, but it's not quite the same as the first one you had."

Just prior to game time came the news that Pelle Lindbergh would be replaced by Bob Froese as the Flyers' starting netminder. Lindbergh was suffering from a tendon problem in his right knee and Keenan decided not to risk further injury by playing the Swede.

The general feeling in Northlands Coliseum prior to the game was one of guarded optimism. Nobody in town was willing to bet a plug nickel on Philadelphia's chances of extending the series, but the Flyers had quickly made it clear they would not roll over and die. What everyone quickly discovered, however, was that Edmonton had both the desire and the ability to take matters into its own hand, regardless of the opposition. As a result, Game 5 ended – to all intents and purposes – shortly after it began.

While operating smoothly and efficiently on all cylinders, the magnificent Oiler machine tore an irreparable swath through the Flyer defence *en route* to building a huge 4-1 advantage in the first period. The onslaught began at the 4:54 mark, when Jari Kurri finally busted his personal scoring slump by taking Gretzky's pass and picking the far corner on Froese. The goal was Kurri's first of the series and 19th of the playoffs, tying a post-season record set by Philadelphia's Reg Leach nine years earlier.

Less than a minute later, Willy Kindstrom slid a 20-footer past Froese for a 2-0 Oiler lead and sent Northlands Coliseum into a frenzy. Rich Sutter briefly interrupted the rout when he scored the Flyers' first goal at 7:23, but Paul Coffey seriously damaged Philadelphia's comeback plans with two markers of his own – in a 2:26 span – late in the period.

While setting up Coffey's first goal, Gretzky made everyone's head swim. He pulled to his forehand at the Flyer blueline, faked defenceman Miroslav Dvorak inside, and then feathered an immaculate back-hand feed to Coffey who flipped the puck over a helpless Froese. It was truly one of the most exquisite moves of all time.

When Mark Messier and Mike Krushelnyski added to the Oiler margin with goals 62 seconds apart halfway through the middle period, the party was on. The Oilers' official cheerleader – who had been prancing in and about the spectators throughout all three games – played a loud recorded chant of "THE CUP STAYS HERE", and he soon had all 17,000 fans joining in. Gretzky finished off a spectacular three-way passing play at 16:49 and the Oilers led 7-1 after two periods.

The Oilers spent much of the third frame trying to get Kurri his record-breaking 20th goal of the playoffs. The fabulous Finn came close several times but could not beat Froese. Messier sandwiched his second marker of the night between Philadelphia goals by Brian Propp and Rich Sutter – early in the third period – and the Northlands crowd prepared itself for the big celebration.

With 4:38 remaining, the Oilers ahead 8-3, Philadelphia defenceman Brad Marsh and Oiler forward Kevin McClelland began throwing punches in front of the Flyer bench. Obviously frustrated by the Oiler romp, Marsh then whaled away at Edmonton's Don Jackson.

Philadelphia enforcer Dave Brown – dressed for the first time in the series – joined in on the mêlée and Sather began shouting words in Keenan's direction. When the fracas subsided, Marsh grabbed a pair of Oiler gloves and heaved them twenty rows up into the stands. It marked the first real serious outbreak of violence in the series.

Following up on my pre-series oath, I spent the next three minutes trying to find an appropriate vantage point to witness the Stanley Cup presentation. I vainly attempted to wriggle into the alleyway beside the Oiler bench, but I was promptly intercepted by NHL security personnel. After being similarly shooed away from the Flyer aisle, I found a neat little spot on a stairway, about 15 rows in back of the Philadelphia bench. There, unobstructed, I could feel the exhilaration that surrounded me.

As the final 30 seconds ticked off the clock, the entire crowd was on its feet – and roaring! When the sport-timer, high above center-ice, hit "0:00", the frenzied throng let loose with a thunderous howl like I had never heard before. The Oiler players flew off the bench and gathered in a delirious scrum around Fuhr. As I sat and watched the pandemonium unfold, a slight shiver went through my spine.

At the opposite end of the rink, a hoard of photographers marched onto the ice and fought for position around a small podium at the blueline. Seconds later, Hall of Fame curator Lefty Reid appeared through the same exit with the Stanley Cup and another tumultuous roar enveloped the entire arena. For the second time in 53 weeks, Wayne Gretzky meandered through the mob of fans and photographers to accept hockey's ultimate prize from President Ziegler. Roof-raising roar No. 3 reverberated through the Coliseum when the Oiler captain hoisted the Cup high over his head.

Surrounded by a crush of photographers, Gretzky had trouble finding a small path of ice for a victory lap. But he soon broke free of the swarm and joined his mates in a triumphant skate around the rink. Passing the Cup to one another, the Oilers danced to their dressing room, with Messier carefully delivering the coveted trophy.

As the players left the ice, it was announced over the P.A. system that Gretzky had been named winner of the Conn Smythe Trophy. Once again, the people stood and screamed. Within 30 seconds, the Oiler dressing room was a mass of wall-to-wall humanity. The CBC and CTV television crews were busy sharing Oiler players for post-game interviews as the bubbly flowed freely about the crowd.

Intelligent media wags decided to avoid the dressing room crush, and a group of them gathered around a nearby TV set to obtain quotes. Over at the interview area, Sather and Grant Fuhr held court with reporters. While Fuhr was enjoying a bottle of champagne, Sather spoke of the elation he felt. "It's been a great year for us and for our team and the players," beamed the man who had won two Stanley Cups and had guided a Canadian Team – comprised primarily of Oiler players – to the Canada Cup championship, all within twelve months. "The emotional highs we've gone through this year will be something this organization will remember for an awful long time. It's been very exciting for me, but the real exciting part is watching the players react. I enjoy the players so much and seeing them achieve the goals they've been shooting for gives me a great feeling."

As far as the Conn Smythe Trophy went, Sather would not single out Gretzky for his contribution to the team. "If I say Wayne was the difference, then I'm slighting both Grant and Paul, and I'm not going to do that. In a situation like this, I think the Smythe Trophy should be split down the middle. I would have given it to all three of those guys and I would have given Mark Messier a big hunk of it as well. He took every faceoff that was important for our hockey club. No one guy was the distinct difference."

With two Stanley Cups to the Oilers' credit, the word "dynasty" crept into the questioning. "I don't understand that cliché," Sather quipped.

After accepting the Smythe Trophy on all three TV networks, Gretzky pranced over to the interview area carrying a bottle of champagne. He and Sather embraced happily at the table and the Great One spoke, first, about winning the Smythe. "It was a tremendous thrill, but from my heart I wish I could put Paul Coffey's name next to mine," he began. "He is such a tremendous help to me and everything I accomplish, and I honestly feel either one of us could have won it. It must have been the closest vote in the history of the award."

Gretzky then compared his current feelings to those after the first Cup victory the previous year. "In terms of emotion and excitement, No. 1 was bigger," he admitted. "But to do what we had to do to win the Cup twice – well, we proved a lot of things to the entire hockey world. And I'll say the same thing now that I said last year – it's going to take a darn good team to take it away from us. As far as I'm concerned, we've got to be rated as good as any team that ever won two in a row. All I know is that 15 years from now, I'm going to say 'Gawd, I played on a great hockey team!'"

The Flyer dressing room was understandably low-key, but there was also an up-beat feeling among the players. Despite losing their first bid for the Stanley Cup, they truly believed in their chances for returning to the Finals. "We'll be back," vowed Rich Sutter, who sat alone, tears streaming down his face. "No one is pointing fingers in here. They were better than us... this time. It's a learning experience. Be honest: did anyone expect us to be here at the beginning of the season? I think every single player in this room has a lot to be proud of and absolutely nothing to be ashamed of. See my head? I'm holding it high."

General manager Bob Clarke, who captained the Flyers to those two Stanley Cups in the mid-70s, made no excuses for losing this time around. "We were beaten by a great hockey club but that doesn't take the lustre off a great season," he said. "Nobody has as many skilled players as the Edmonton Oilers. We have a helluva team, but they're better. I think they proved that beyond a doubt."

After showering, Flyer defenceman Brad Marsh was back to his jolly, good-natured self. Joking with reporters, he was asked why he tossed those two Oiler gloves into the audience during the late-game scrap. "Those people pay good money for those seats. They deserve a souvenir," he cracked.

Outside the Coliseum, word of the championship victory had spread to the streets, and car horns were blaring throughout the city. Traffic heading towards downtown was at a virtual standstill as Cup revellers began their assault on the town. For a nine-block stretch along Jasper Avenue, Oiler fans – many of them inebriated - created a massive outdoor mall as they marched from one end to another, hooting, hollering, blowing horns, and chanting "We're Number One!"

Edmonton police blocked off traffic along Jasper and kept a close eye on the proceedings. I introduced myself to one officer seated in a police van at the corner of Jasper and 100th Street, and he asked me if I had suicidal tendencies. Before heeding his advice and heading back up to my hotel room, I asked if the celebration was reaching the previous year's level of lunacy. "I think it'll be worse than that before it's over," he said. "These people walk the nine blocks and then turn around and come right back. They do circuits. I wouldn't be surprised if this went on till five or six in the morning." The cop wasn't too far off in his prediction. After more than five hours of prancing, the mob finally broke up and went home to nurse its collective hangover at around 4:30 a.m.

Three days later, on a warm and windy Sunday afternoon, more than 4,000 Edmontonians lined a 10-block parade route to watch the Oilers wind through downtown with the Cup. Later on, 20,000 more fans cheered wildly from the stands at Commonwealth Stadium as the players circled the outer track in automobiles. As the people stood and clapped for their heroes, a stranger from Toronto couldn't help but wonder how many more times this very scene would be repeated in the future. Dynasty? Don't bet against it.

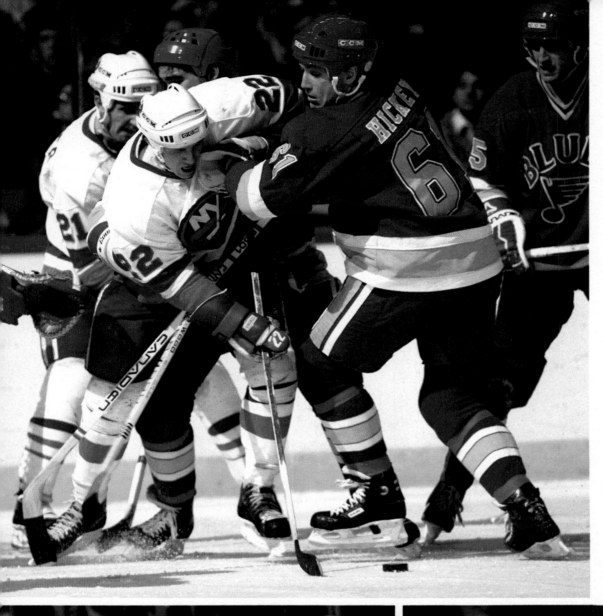

(Previous page) the most dominant figure in current-day professional sport: Wayne Gretzky of the two-time defending Stanley Cup champion Edmonton Oilers. (Opposite page, top) Pittsburgh Penguin Doug Shedden looks to set up teammate Mike Bullard in front of New York Islanders' goalie Billy Smith. (Opposite page, bottom) Islanders' sniper Mike Bossy (22) is placed under wraps in front of the New York Rangers' bench. (Left) very few players are feared more than Bossy when there's a loose puck. Here, he battled with St. Louis Blues' veteran forward Pat Hickey in 1984-85 NHL action. (Below, left) sporting the results of a recent tussle, Detroit Red Wings' forward Ron Duguay speeds up ice. (Below, right) the quintessential hockey bad man: St. Louis forward/defenceman Dwight Schofield. "Fighting isn't a glamorous role, but it's my passport to the NHL," he admits. (Overleaf, left) Rangers' James Patrick battles for position with Islanders' Gord Dineen as goalie Kelly Hrudey looks on. (Overleaf, right) Buffalo Sabers' Dave Andreychuk braces himself for a spill as he rounds back of New Jersey Devils' net. Devils' defenceman Dave Pichette awaits his arrival.

(Top) Rick Vaive deflects Pat Hickey's shot past Islanders' goalie Billy Smith in Vaive's first-ever game with the Maple Leafs, February 1980. He scored two goals that night. (Bottom, left) Washington Capitals' rugged, young defenceman Scott Stevens appears ready and willing to notify Mike Bossy that he's around. (Bottom, right) Vaive become Maple Leaf captain in January 1982, following the bitter departure of Darryl Sittler from the Toronto organization.

(Previous page, top) Minnesota's Brian Bellows suffered through a dismal 1984-85 campaign. Some insiders felt he was too young to handle the team captaincy, (Bottom) New Jersey's Kirk Muller distinguished himself as one of the NHL's most proficient penalty killers in his rookie season. Here, he keeps a close eye on Islander point-man Stefan Person. (Left) former Canadiens' forward Mark Hunter positions himself in front of Islander goalie Kelly Hrudey. Hunter was obtained by St. Louis in a complicated deal on draft day, June 1985. (Right) Chicago Black Hawks' sparkplug Denis Savard, the most dazzling and exciting skater in the NHL.

(Bottom, left) Big Tim Kerr scored 54 goals for Philadelphia in 1984-85 and continued to remind the hockey world of former Bruin great Phil Esposito. An injured leg kept him out of action during much of the '84-85 Stanley Cup Final against Edmonton. (Right) a distressing series of lower back difficulties has prevented Calgary defenceman Paul Reinhart from attaining his full potential. No Flame, however, plays better in the big games against Edmonton. (Overleaf, left) Winnipeg Jets' center Dale Hawerchuk became a bonafide superstar in 1984-85 and the club awarded him with a $3 million contract. (Right) Boston's wheelhorse on defence, Raymond Bourque, placed runner-up to Edmonton's Paul Coffey in balloting for the 1984-85 Norris Trophy.

(Right) no defenceman in the past 10 years has resembled the immortal Bobby Orr quite as closely as Edmonton's Paul Coffey. Widely regarded as the most gifted skater in the NHL, Coffey's blend of speed, strength, and intelligence is a major reason behind the Oilers' smashing success. (Bottom, left) traded from Chicago to the Vancouver Canucks in 1982, winger Tony Tanti has become the most prolific goalscorer in the 15-year history of the Smythe Division team. Here, he is watched closely by Islanders' defenceman Denis Potvin. (Right) although he has averaged more than 80 points per season throughout his career with St. Louis Blues, center Bernie Federko remains among the most under-rated players in the NHL.

(Right) the New Jersey Devils' franchise has been most transient in NHL history. It began in 1974-75 as the Kansas City Scouts and become Colorado Rockies (in Denver) in 1976-77. Houston Astros' baseball owner John McMullen purchased the Rockies and moved the team to the Meadowlands Sports Complex at East Rutherford, N.J. in 1982, re-naming it the Devils. Here, forward Aaron Broten is harassed by Los Angeles defenceman Craig Redmond during 1984-85 action against the Kings. Goaltender Bob Janecyk watches the play.

In the only professional sport where fighting is an acceptable element, (top) Philadelphia's Joe Paterson is restrained from yanking Kirk Muller's sweater. (Above, left) Devils' Bob MacMillan high-sticks Leaf defenceman. (Right) blood trickles down face of Jim Nill. (Opposite, top) rival Rangers and Islanders wrestle. (Opposite, bottom) Devils and Sabers do a little dance.

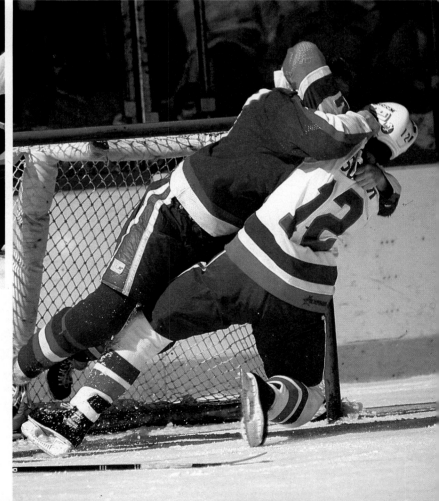

(Previous page, left) Rangers' Barry Beck is sandwiched by two St. Louis players. (Right) Islanders' John Tonelli is wrestled to the ice by Flyers' rearguard Brad Marsh as linesman Wayne Bonney intercedes. (Opposite) Bruins and Devils do battle late in 1984-85. Steve Kasper tussles with Pat Verbeek in main event. (Top) Islanders and Canadiens gather in hockey version of a rugger scrum as Guy Carbonneau looks for an opening. (Above) can the puck be somewhere beneath this pile of Islanders and Canucks? (Right) Winnipeg defenceman Randy Carlyle attacks Islanders Duane Sutter, who looks ready.

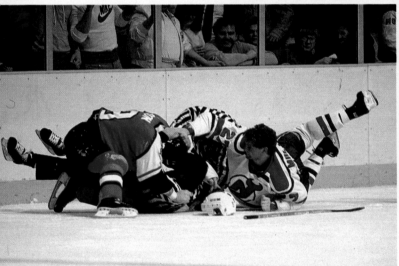

(Opposite, top) Rangers' Don Maloney keeps an eye on Quebec's Mario Marois as Nordiques and Blueshirts exchange greetings. (Bottom) Ranger Warren Miller watches from below during Toronto/New York disagreement. (Top) goalie Billy Smith assists defender Denis Potvin in clearing Vancouver players from Islander goalcrease. (Above) Devils' Kirk Muller introduces Flyer Joe Paterson to linesman. (Right) Ex-Flyer Ken Linseman (now with Boston) glares menacingly at ex-Ranger Eddie Johnstone.

(Opposite, top) Referee Ron Hoggarth helps linesman settle Flyer/Devil feud. (Bottom) Rangers' Nick Fotiu (center) appears upset as benches empty against St. Louis. (Left) Islanders' Mats Hallin goes scurrying for a Kleenex. (Below) Former Bruin defenceman Mike Milbury makes one final point before leaving ice for repairs in New Jersey. (Bottom) Islander goalie Kelly Hrudey sprinted the length of the ice to encounter Ranger netminder John Vanbiesbrouck.

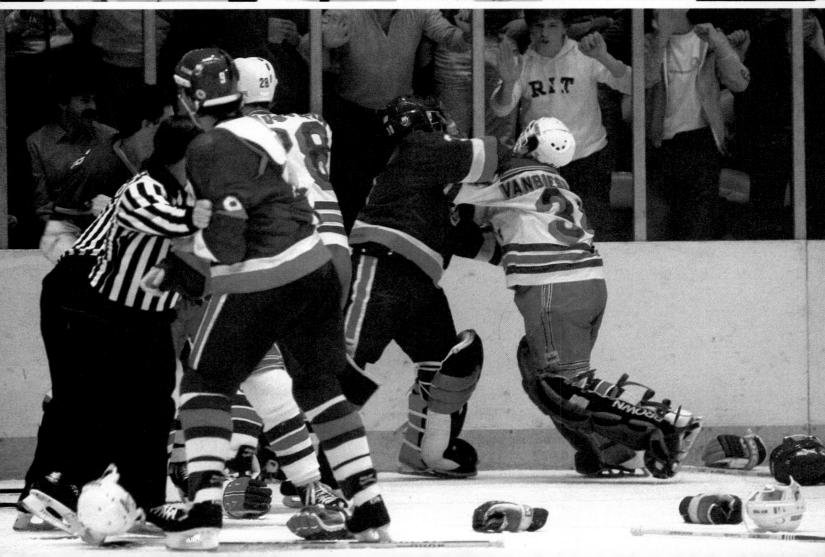

(Left) Big David Babych is a menacing figure along the blueline for the Winnipeg Jets — one of the NHL's most improved teams in 1984-85. His brother, Wayne, is a former 50-goals shooter with St. Louis who played with Pittsburgh last season. (Right) forward Ron Sutter (14) and identical-twin brother Rich both play for the Philadelphia Flyers. In all, there are six Sutter brothers in the NHL. The eldest, Brian, plays for St. Louis. Darryl plays for Chicago, while Brent (below, left) and Duane (below, right) both toil for the Islanders. Brent finished 11th in League scoring in 1984-85 with 102 points while playing on a forward unit with Mike Bossy and John Tonelli. The line was born during the 1984 Canada Cup Tournament, following center Bryan Trottier's decision to play for the U.S.A. team. Darryl Sutter's 1984-85 highlight was his overtime goal that eliminated Minnesota North Stars in the Norris Division playoff final.

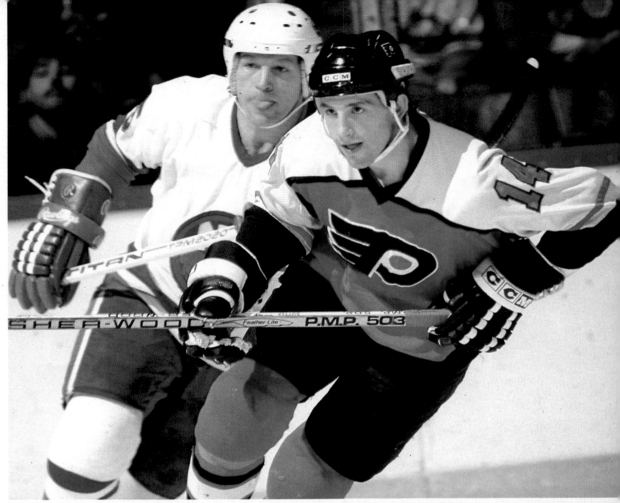

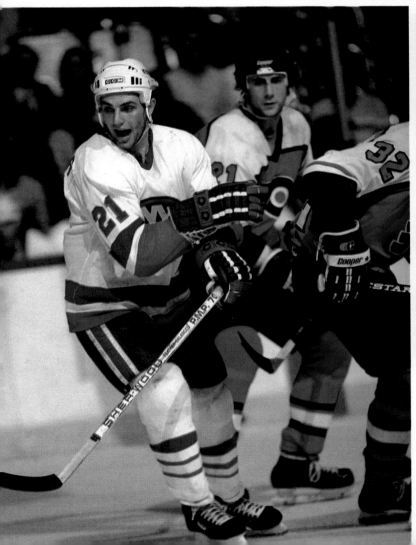

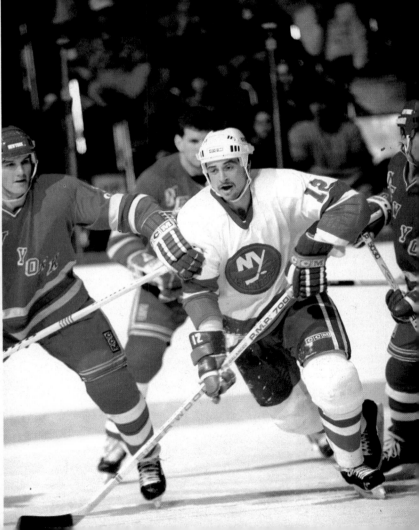

(Left) Rich Sutter, identical brother of Ron, was traded to the Flyers from Pittsburgh — the team that drafted him in 1982. (Above) Pittsburgh's phenomenal center Mario Lemieux was the highest-touted draft choice to enter the NHL since Guy Lafleur in 1971. Lemieux deservedly won the Calder Trophy as the NHL's top rookie in 1984-85. Wayne Babych — David's brother and Lemieux's linemate in Pittsburgh — is in the background. (Opposite page) brothers Kevin Dineen (Hartford, top left) and Gord Dineen (Islanders, bottom left) began to exert themselves in 1984-85. Kevin scored 25 goals for the Whalers while Gord was a +10 on defence for the Islanders. Vancouver forward Patrik Sundstrom (top right) slowed down a bit in '84-85 but still led the punchless Canucks in scoring with 68 points. The Maloney brothers (Dave and Don) were split up when defenceman Dave (bottom left) was traded from the Rangers to Buffalo in 1984.

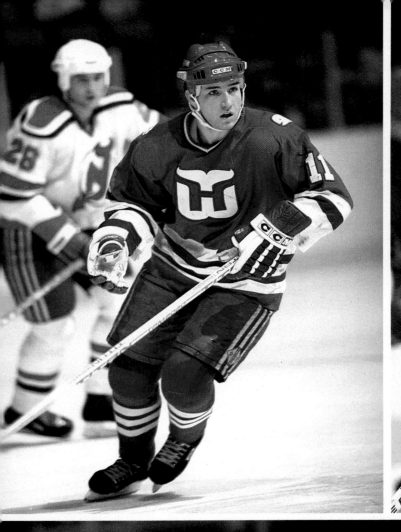

(Left) Chicago goalie Murray Bannerman is one of the few remnants of an era when all goaltenders wore plastic masks. Here, he clears puck away from Ranger Peter Sundstrom (25). (Right) the majority of NHL netminders now wear caged face-guards attached to plastic helmets. Islanders' Kelly Hrudey shelters puck from Buffalo forward Sean McKenna. (Below, left) Despite his advanced years, New Jersey goalie Glenn (Chico) Resch, still among the League's quickest and smartest, kicks out a shot as team-mate Phil Russell watches. (Below, right) after leading the Islanders to four consecutive Stanley Cups, veteran Billy Smith's workload dwindled in 1984-85 as youngster Kelly Hrudey assumed the No. 1 position on the team. Still, there are few goalies in NHL history who performed better in the clutch than did Smith in his prime.

Ex-Canadien Rick Wamsley (upper left) is now with St. Louis. Did he close his pads in time to save this one? Rangers' Glen Hanlon (upper right) extends his right arm for balance to make a stop. Bob Janycek (left) of Los Angeles sprawls to his left to prevent a goal. (Opposite, top) New Jersey defenceman Bob Hoffmeyer attempts to clear puck as Winnipeg's Doug Smail (9) and Laurie Boschman close in. (Bottom) Vancouver's Richard Brodeur is about to be victimized by Islanders' Mike Bossy in 1981-82 Stanley Cup Final.

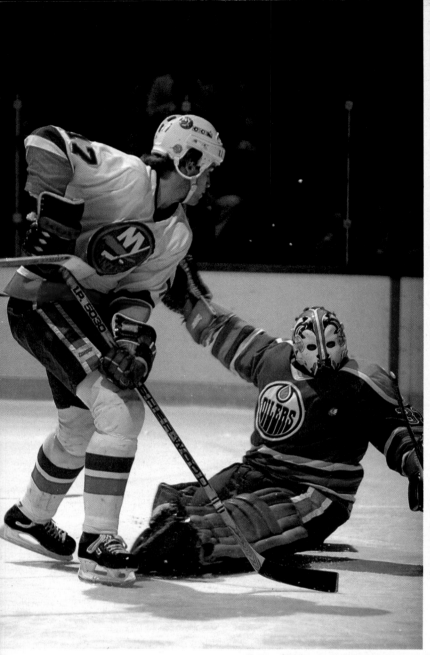

(Upper, left) Oilers' Grant Fuhr makes arm save on Islanders' Greg Gilbert. St. Louis goalie Mike Liut (upper right) — now with Hartford — shoots puck away from Devils' player. (Right) Richard Brodeur gloves a hard shot as the ever-dangerous Bossy lingers close. (Opposite, top) Islander winger John Tonelli flips backhand shot over Buffalo's Tom Barrasso. (Bottom, left) Washington's Al Jensen is about to be drilled in a tender spot! (Bottom, right) Pete Peeters of Boston juggles hard shot but keeps it out.

(Left) Washington defenceman Scott Stevens (3) is in hot water with three Islander players as he ventures a little too close to goalie Billy Smith. (Right) Calgary defenceman Al MacInnis floors ex-Islander Anders Kallur with a right jab. Kallur, who once scored 36 goals, was released by the Isles in July, 1985. (Bottom, left) Boston's Keith Crowder looks none too amused as he's bounced rudely to the ice by former Islander Billy Corroll — now with Edmonton. (Bottom, right) Washington forward Gaetan Duchesne is not about to let Islanders' Pat LaFontaine sneak past him along the boards. A former American Olympian, LaFontaine did not quite live up to expectations in his first full year with the Islanders.

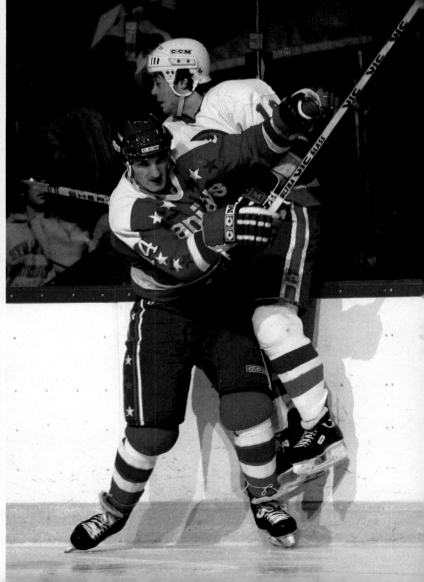

(Top) Islander John Tonelli uses Penguin goalie Michel Dion as an easy chair. (Left) New Jersey's Joe Cirella drops down to block a shot against the Islanders. (Above) Bossy completes hat-trick against Vancouver in '81-82 Cup Final. (Opposite, top) Toronto's Dan Daoust sprawls to help thwart Devils' threat. (Bottom) defenceman Ken Morrow (left) and Denis Potvin of the Islanders clear Penguin forwards from goalcrease.

(Left) Quebec's Wilf Paiement (27) backhands shot towards Montreal goalie Steve Penney as Larry Robinson (19) defends. (Opposite, bottom) Islanders' netminder Billy Smith pins Devils' Joe Cirella while defenceman Gord Dineen guards open cage. (Right) New Jersey's Rich Preston pays a visit to former Chicago teammate Murray Bannerman. Hawk defencemen Bob Murray (6) and Doug Wilson look on. (Bottom, left) John Tonelli sails over fallen Ranger rearguard Barry Beck. (Bottom, right) Devils' John MacLean appears to be coordinating a dance step with screened Islander goalie Billy Smith. Music anyone?

(Opposite, top) Montreal goalie Steve Penney smothers puck as Quebec's Andre Savard (12) and Peter Stastny look for rebound. (Opposite, bottom) Nordiques' Tony McKegney dives to avoid fallen Islander goalie Billy Smith. (Below) Buffalo's Mike Foligno is hammered to the ice by Devils' rearguard Dave Pichette. (Right) Penguins' Randy Hillier puts the wraps on Islander forward Greg Gilbert. (Bottom) wide angle view of 1985 action between the Canadiens and Whalers at the Hartford Civic Center.

(Left) Montreal defenceman Jean Hamel asks Islander winger Clark Gillies to excuse himself from the Canadiens' goalcrease. (Bottom, left) Gillies and ex-Canuck Harold Snepsts struggle for position in front of Vancouver net. (Bottom, right) New Jersey's Paul Gagne celebrates goal he has just scored on Islanders' Billy Smith. Smith appears ready to celebrate slash at Gagne's leg. (Opposite, top) Islander players gather around Smith after what appears to be a losing effort (note the expressions). (Bottom) Vancouver players Neil Belland (15), Stan Smyl (12), Jim Nill (8), Rick Heinz, and Curt Fraser gather to congratulate goaltender Richard Brodeur after victory.

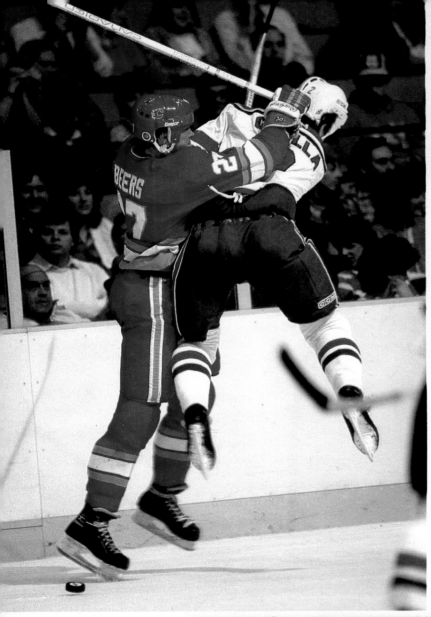

(Opposite, clockwise from left)
Islander Greg Gilbert
celebrates goal against
Montreal in 1984 playoffs.
Flyers' defenceman Brad
Marsh sprawls to protect net
as goalie Pelle Lindbergh
watches puck sail wide by
inches. Ranger James Patrick
becomes entangled with
Islander Denis Potvin in 1984-
85 action on Long Island.
Bird's eye view of action
between the Islanders and
Philadelphia from the Nassau
Coliseum. (Above, left) Fans
watch both pensively and with
amusement as Devils' Joe
Cirella crashes into Calgary
forward Eddy Beers. (Above,
right) Mike Bossy wiggles free
of Ranger defenceman Tom
Laidlaw. (Right) Ranger
forward Mark Pavelich is
swatted aside by Islander
goalie Billy Smith.

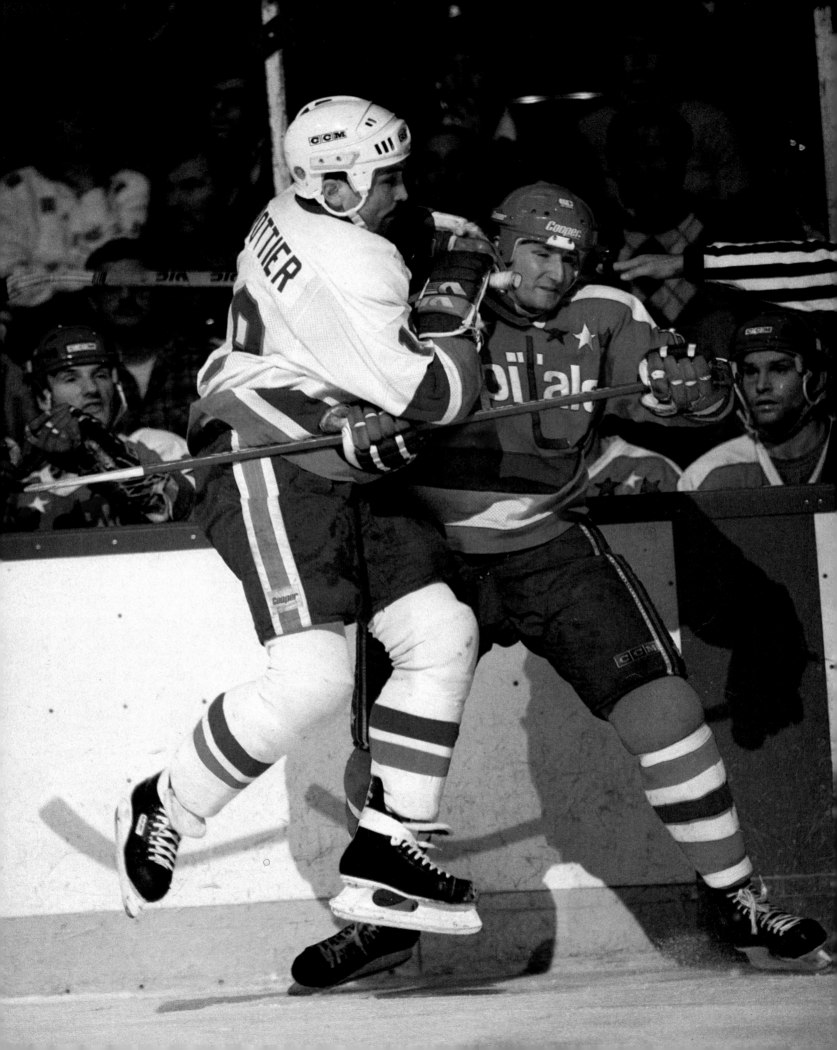

(Left) Islanders' center Bryan Trottier struggles free of Washington checker Darren Veitch during game at Nassau Coliseum. Trottier surprised many Canadiens when he chose to play for Team U.S.A. in the 1984 Canada Cup tournament. It turned out to be a costly move as Islander coach Al Arbour replaced Trottier with Brent Sutter on the club's first line (with John Tonelli and Mike Bossy). The latter unit was put together by Team Canada. (Overleaf) the linesmen move in to squelch a disagreement between New Jersey's Joe Cirella (left) and Hartford's Ray Neufeld as Devils' captain Mel Bridgman acts as peace maker.

(Left) Defenceman Denis Potvin — the Islanders' team captain — goes falling backwards over teammate Billy Smith. Both players were key elements in the Isles' string of four consecutive Stanley Cups between 1979-80 and 1982-83. (Bottom, left) Minnesota North Stars' Dennis Maruk pauses prior to faceoff against the Rangers. Maruk began his NHL career in 1975 with the now-defunct California Golden Seals. He has also played in Cleveland and Washington. (Bottom, right) Calgary defenceman Dave Hanson squeezes Devils' forward Aaron Broten into boards at the Byrne Meadowlands Arena.

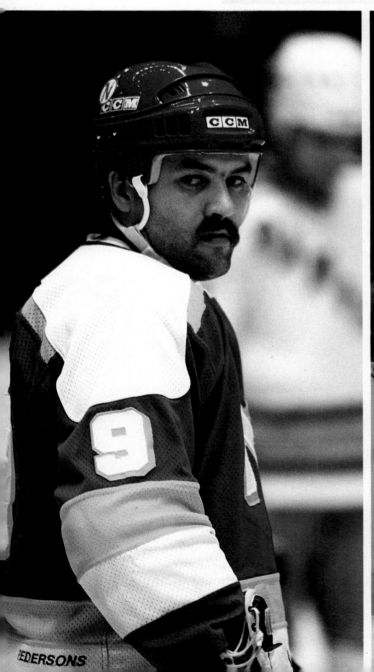

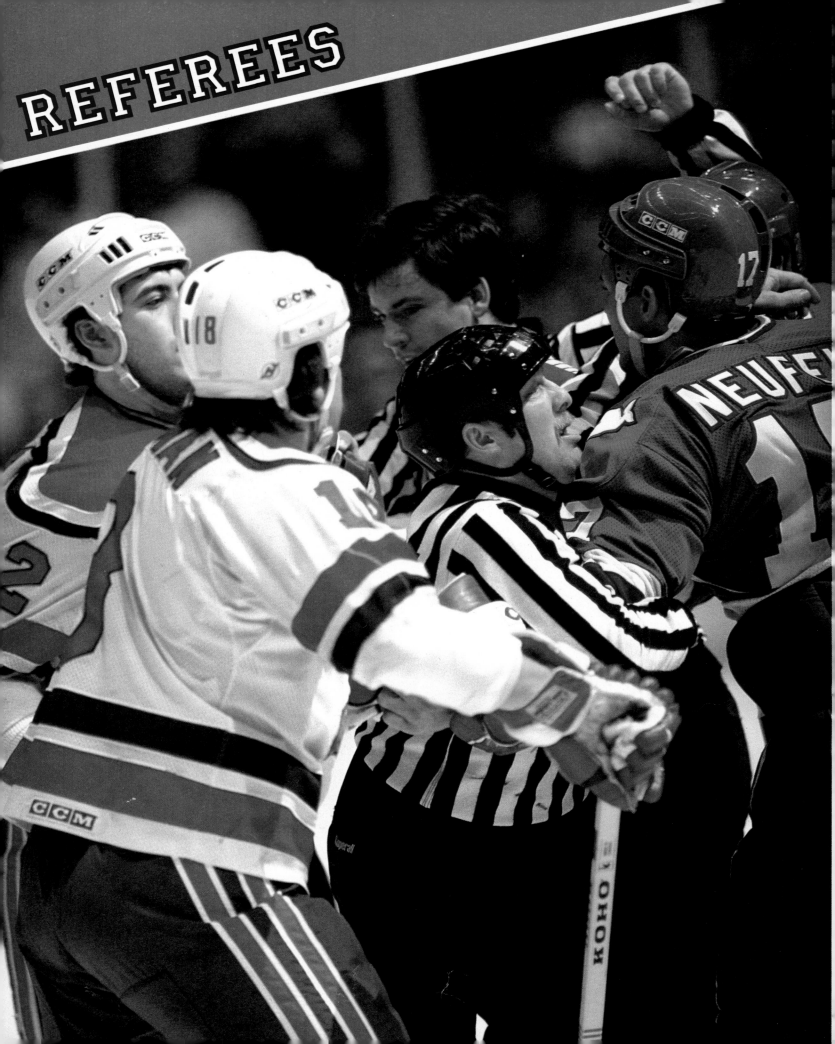

(Left) Linesman Wayne Bonney (left) and Dan Schacte break up fight between Rangers George McPhee and Washington player. (Below) Islander Bob Nystrom and Flyer Dave Brown finish disagreement as referee Bryan Lewis issues warning. (Bottom) Norris Division rivals Chicago and Minnesota discuss proceedings.

(Left) Linesman Ray Scapinello looks for an opening so he can separate ex-Ranger Eddie Johnstone from Flyers' captain (and now GM) Bobby Clarke. (Bottom, left) Referee Bruce Hood is amused over something during game involving the defunct Colorado Rockies. Hood became the first referee to handle 1,000 regular-season NHL games before retiring after the 1983-84 season. He is currently writing an autobiography about his experiences in the big league. (Bottom, right) referee Dave Newell raises his left arm to signal a penalty in game between Detroit and New Jersey. A back injury forced Newell to sit out the latter portion of the 1984-85 season as well as the entire playoffs. (Right) the Flyers and Islanders have another difference of opinion. (Below) St. Louis captain Brian Sutter (left) is separated from ex-Ranger Scott Kleinendorst (now with Hartford).

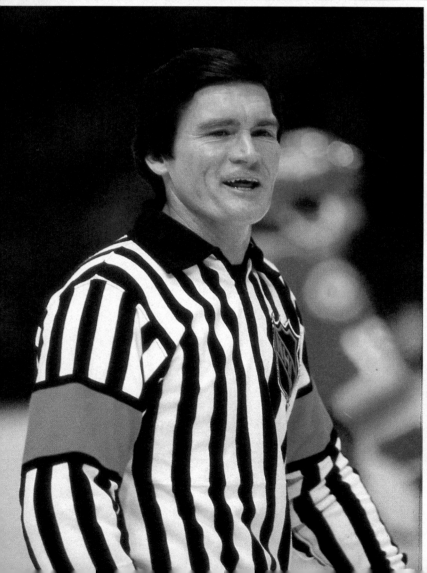

(Right) Bird's-eye view of confrontation between Islanders' Ken Morrow and Edmonton's Dave Hunter. Wayne Gretzky, meanwhile, keeps an eye on Brent Sutter. (Bottom, left) referee Kerry Fraser calls a holding penalty against Oilers' Hunter during game 4 of the 1984-85 Stanley Cup Final. (Bottom, right) veteran referee Ron Wicks points Whaler defenceman Ulf Samuelsson towards the penalty box. (Opposite page) two photos of Stanley Cup Final action involving the Islanders: (top) Bryan Trottier tries to wrestle Vancouver's Tiger Williams away from Billy Smith during '82 Final; (bottom) linesman Ray Scapinello steps in to prevent an outbreak between Islander Clark Gillies and North Star players Neal Broten (left) and Paul Shmyr during '81 championship series.

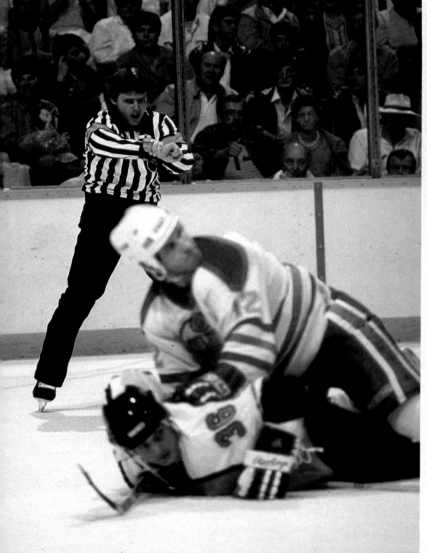

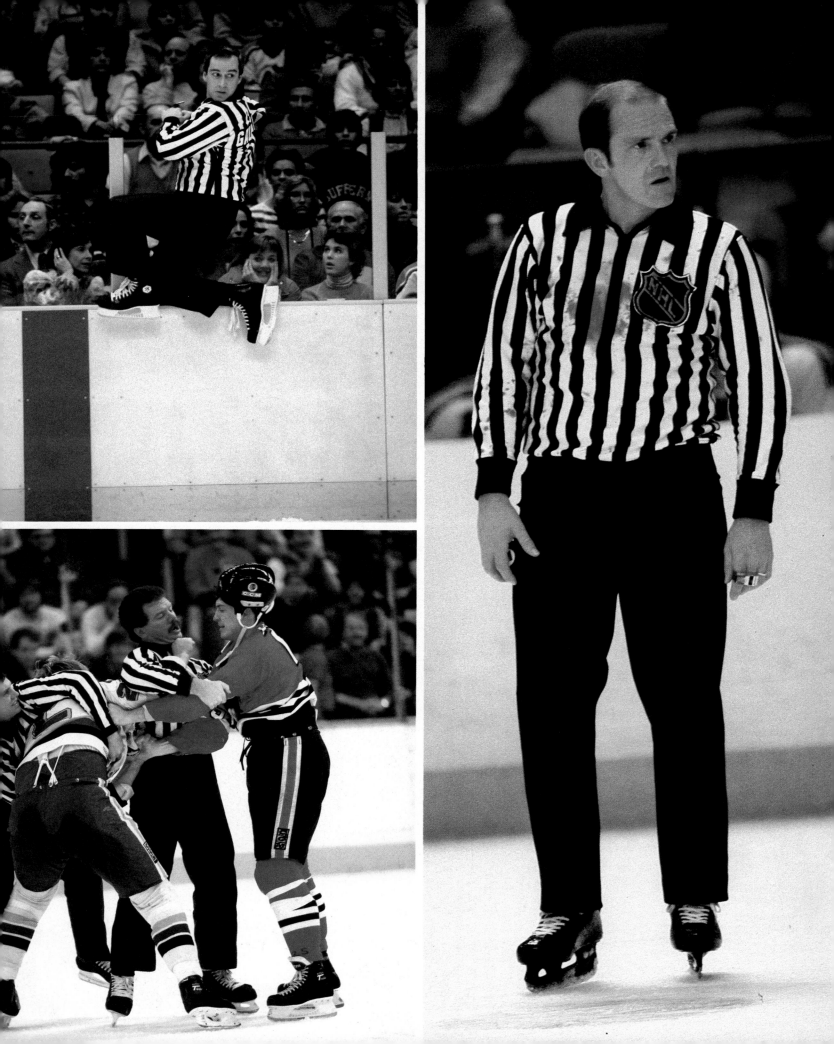

(Opposite, top left) linesman Gerard Gauthier obviously wants no part of whatever or whomever is coming towards him. (Bottom, left) linesman Randy Mitton grabs arm of Chicago's Jerome Dupont in battle against Minnesota's Willie Plett. (Left) Sometimes, breaking up a fight is a pretty messy proposition as veteran linesman Bob Hodges will attest. One of the combatants he dealt with obviously took a shot in the snout. (Above) referee Brian Lewis executes a perfect slide into second base; only, this is hockey! Lewis fell to the ice during action between the Islanders and Oilers in the 1983-84 Stanley Cup Final. (Right) referee Ron Hoggarth arbitrates a hearing between Islanders' Dave Langevin (left) and former Ranger captain Dave Maloney (now with Buffalo). Never a dull moment!

THE OILERS & GRETZKY

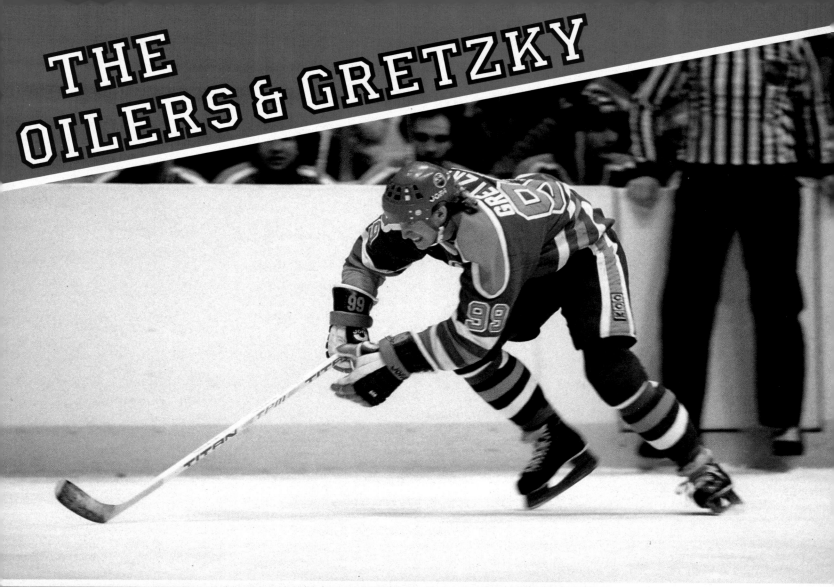

There is much debate, these days, whether or not Wayne Gretzky is the greatest hockey player who ever lived. His few detractors stop short of making such a claim by including Gordie Howe, Bobby Orr, Maurice (Rocket) Richard, Jean Beliveau, and Bobby Hull in the same category. One thing, however, is for certain: no player in the history of pro hockey has ever exerted quite as big an impact on the game. Gretzky's face is among the most recognizable of any North American celebrity and he has even appeared as an actor on an episode of *The Young And The Restless.* These photos display Gretzky's agility and intensity. Always in position near the net, he is watched closely by Devils' goalie Glenn Resch (opposite, upper left) and is thwarted at point-blank range (right) by Islander netminder Billy Smith during the 1984 Stanley Cup Final.

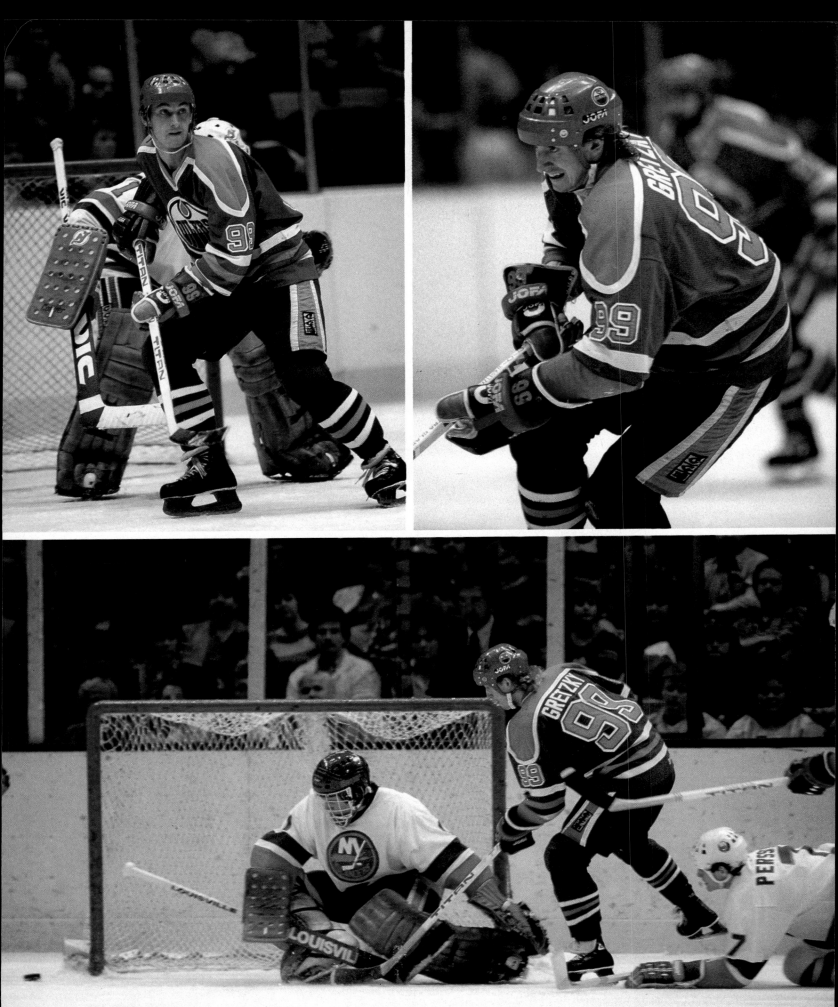

The Oilers are hockey's Team of the 1980s. With two consecutive Stanley Cups to its credit, the club has revolutionized the sport with its unique brand of rapid puck movement. (Opposite top) Paul Coffey congratulates Gretzky after goal as the Oilers relax at bench during time out. (Bottom) goalie Grant Fuhr makes a fine save off Islanders' Anders Kallur as defenceman Kevin Lowe prepares to clear rebound. (Right) Fuhr shoots glove hand to his right but misses this one against the Islanders. (Bottom, left) the most familiar face in North American sport today: Wayne Gretzky. The 24-year-old Brantford, Ont. native became Oiler captain in 1983-84, replacing Lee Fogolin, (Bottom, right) Oilers' Czechoslovak-born winger Jaroslav Pouzar reaches for the puck as linemate Gretzky watches with anticipation.

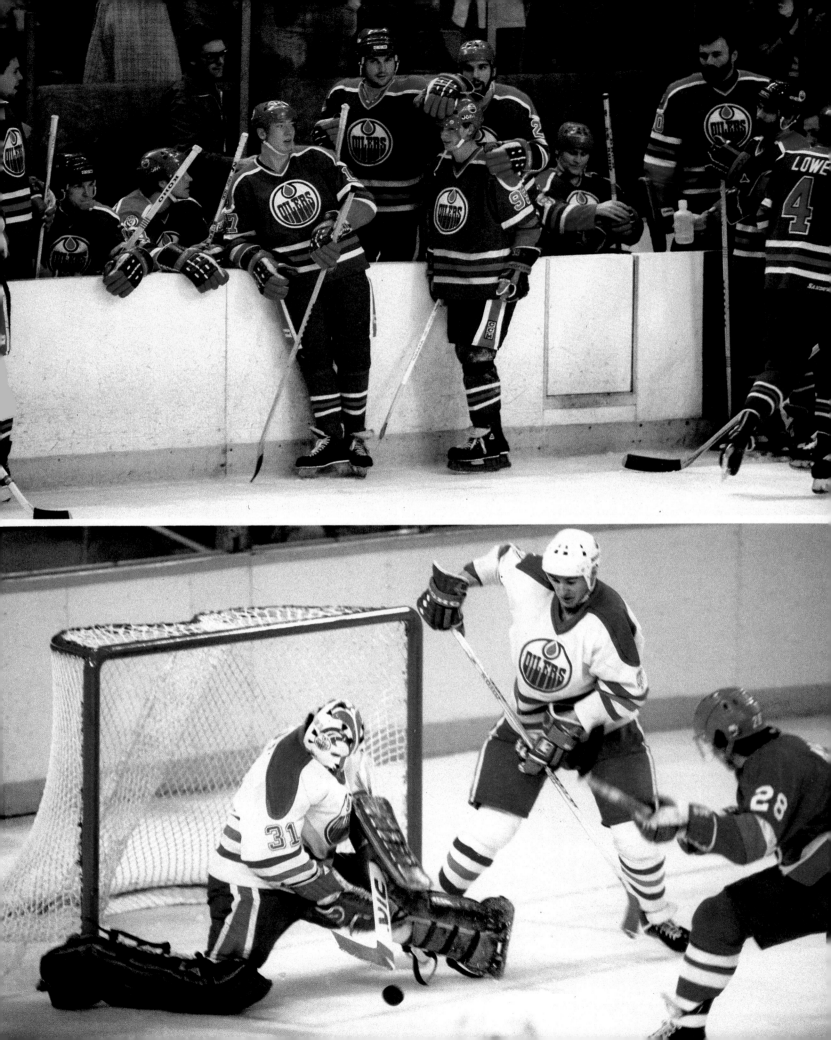

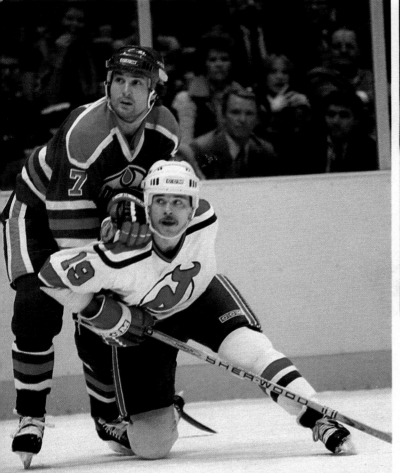

(Opposite page) Oiler forward Glenn Anderson looks for deflection in front of Islander goalie Billy Smith. (Top) Oilers' Mike Krushelnyski is checked tightly by Ranger center Mike Rogers in 1984-85 game at Madison Square Garden. (Left) New Jersey forward Rich Preston looks pleadingly at referee after being pulled down by Paul Coffey. (Above) Krushelnyski wants the puck!

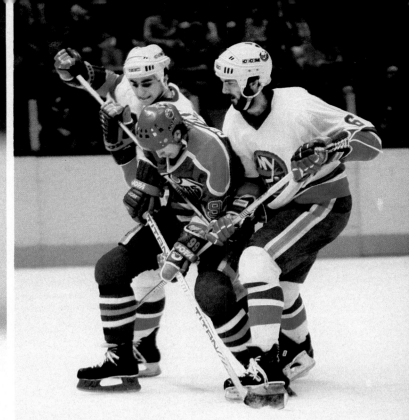

(Opposite, top) Gretzky speeds away from Islander defenceman Ken Morrow, (Bottom) one of the most historic photos in NHL history: Bruce Bennett's shot of Gretzky beating Buffalo goalie Don Edwards for his 77th goal of the 1981-82 season — the goal that broke Phil Esposito's single-season record. Sabers' defenceman Richie Dunn watches helplessly. (Upper, left) Gretzky's utter determination is shown by his strained facial expression. (Upper, right) it often takes more than two players to slow down the Great One. Here, Gretzky appears to be wiggling free of Islanders' Paul Boutilier and Ken Morrow (6). (Right) Gretzky and Ken Linseman congratulate one another after successful scoring effort against New Jersey goalie Glenn Resch. Defenceman Murray Brumwell can only watch. Linseman was traded to Boston in the summer of 1984 for left winger Mike Krushelnyski. The latter scored 43 goals for Edmonton in 1984-85.

(Clockwise from left) Gretzky speeds into position to receive a pass; the Great One leans on his stick during break in the action; New Jersey goalie Glenn Resch has his hands full with the ever-dangerous Gretzky lurking close by. (Opposite, top) Gretzky zooms around Ranger defence for close-in scoring opportunity against goalie Glen Hanlon. (Right) Islander defenceman Dave Langevin (26) appears to be asking teammate Clark Gillies for checking assistance as Gretzky looks for the puck.

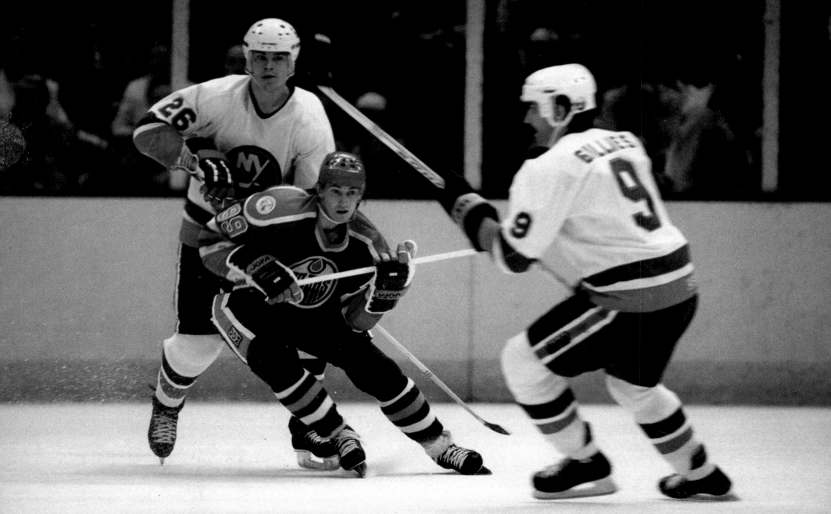

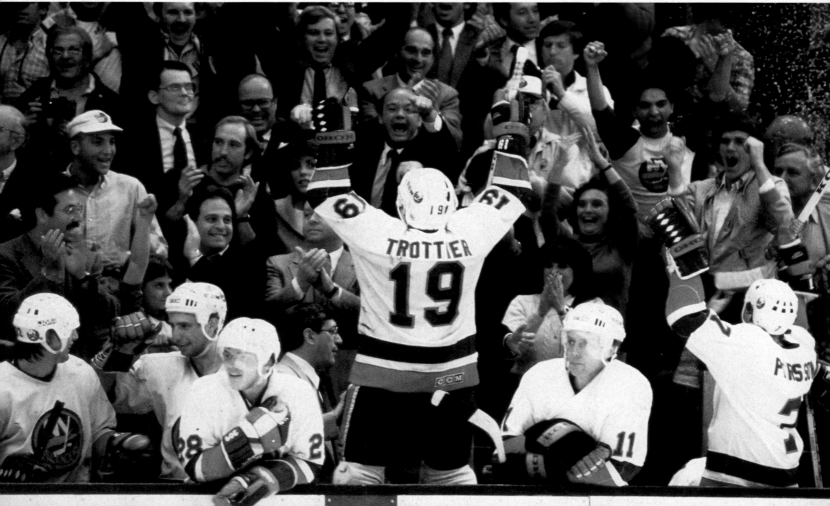

(Opposite, top) after a 13-2 win over New Jersey in 1983, Gretzky called the Devils "a Mickey Mouse team". Here, he makes up with Meadowlands fans by flipping puck into crowd during warm up.

(Bottom) Bryan Trottier leads the cheers as Islanders win fourth Stanley Cup. (Clockwise below) fans in New York, New Jersey and Edmonton (the famous "Flame").

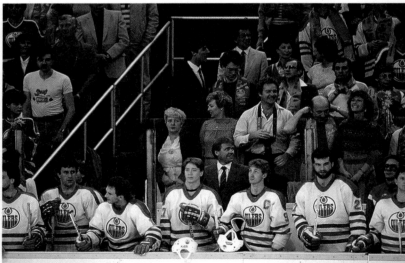

(Top) Islanders and Devils hold a little board meeting. (Left) Gretzky clowns it up with coach Glen Sather (left) and movie stars Goldie Hawn and Burt Reynolds. (Above) Oiler bench seconds before first Stanley Cup victory in 1984. (Opposite top) Islander fans at Nassau Coliseum light sparklers. (Right) Devils and Flyers fight.

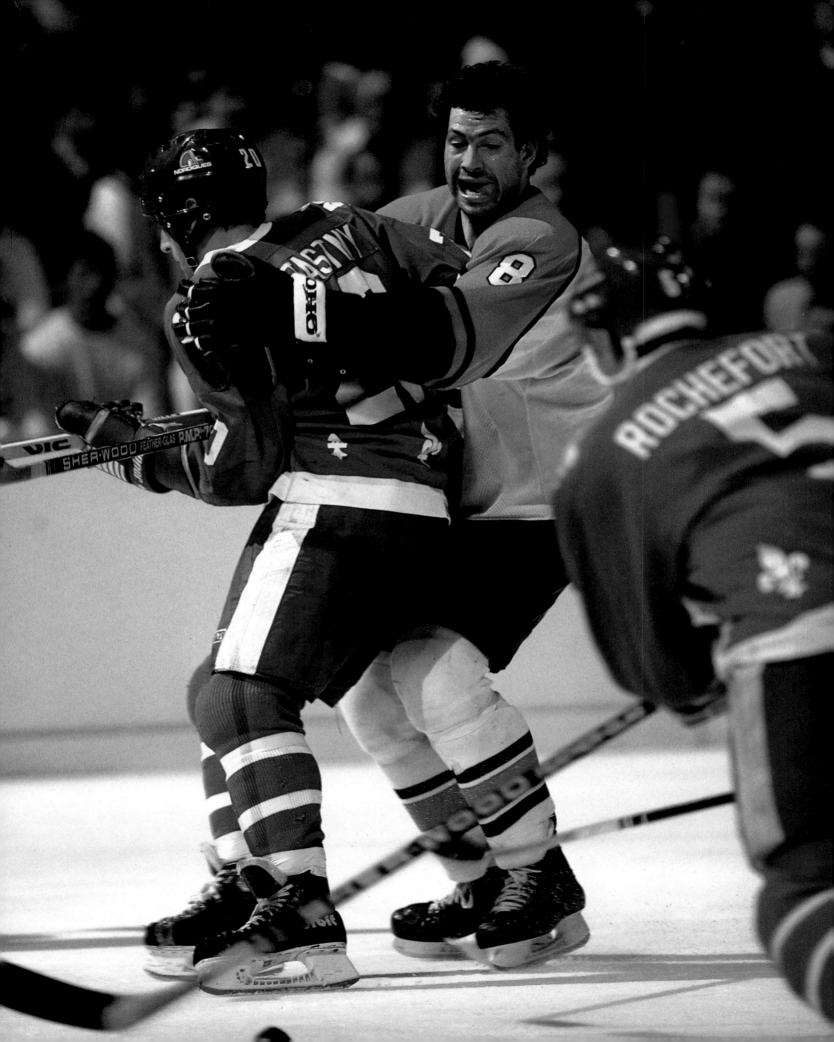

(Previous pages) 1985 playoff action between Quebec and Philadelphia. Mark Howe (2) grabs a hold of Nordiques' Peter Stastny; Brad Marsh (8) puts the wraps on Anton Stastny. (Opposite) Jack O'Callahan of Chicago butt-ends Oiler Mike Krushelnyski in '85 Campbell Conference title series. (This page) more '85 playoff action.

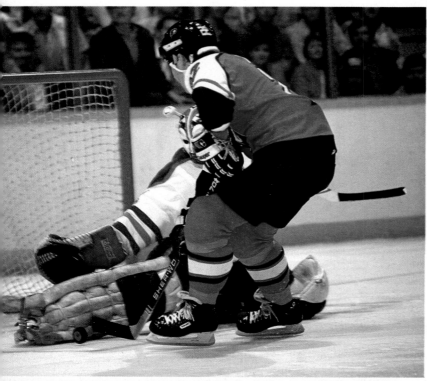

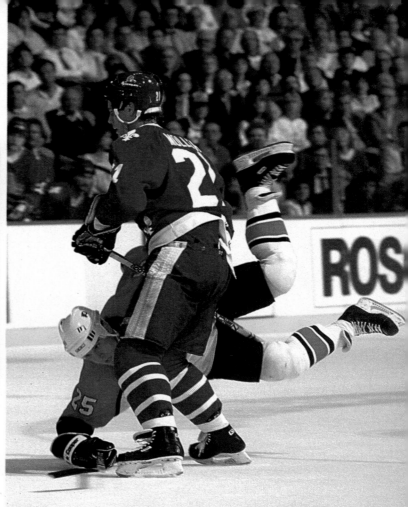

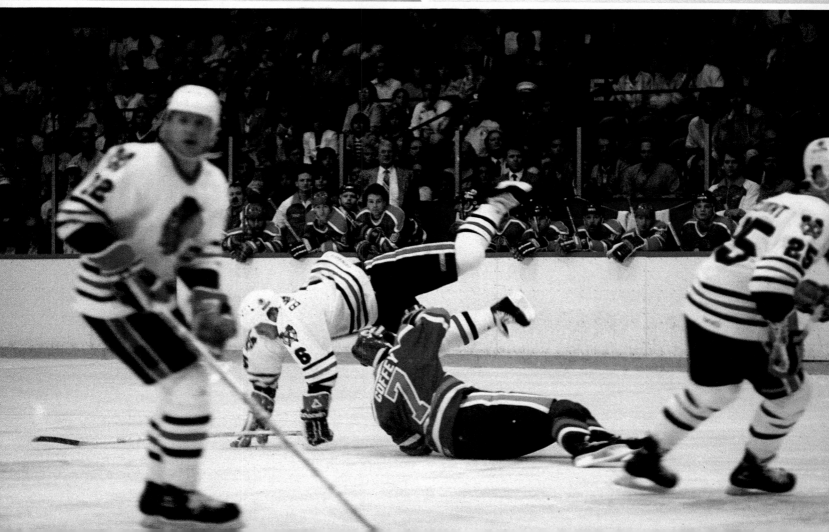

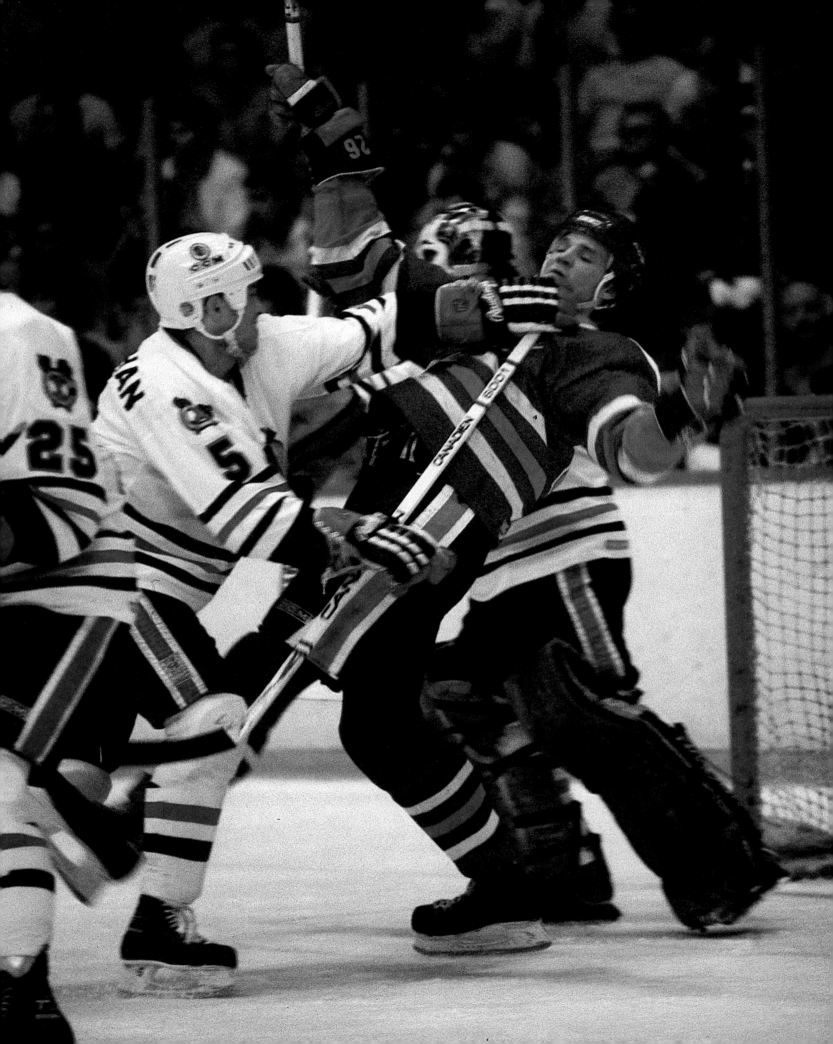

Action from the 1985 Patrick Division playoff final between the Islanders and Philadelphia Flyers. (Opposite top) Flyers' Brian Propp beats goalie Billy Smith on breakaway. (Bottom) a wild scramble in front of Flyer netminder Pelle Lindbergh involves Philly's Brad McCrimmon (10), Mark Howe (2), and Joe Paterson (28) and Islander forwards Bob Bourne and Bryan Trottier (19). (Right) Islanders' veteran defenceman Ken Morrow sends Flyers' superstar Tim Kerr crashing to the ice with classic body check. Kerr missed much of the playoffs with an injured leg. (Bottom left) Trottier tries to take a piece of Flyer rookie forward Rick Tocchet. (Bottom right) John Tonelli plays leap-frog with Flyers' Brian Propp. (Overleaf) Edmonton's Mark Messier steps over fallen Chicago goalie Murray Bannerman; Flyers' Joe Paterson leaps to screen Quebec's Mario Gosselin.

(Upper left) Flyer defenceman Mark Howe is pinned to the boards by Nordiques' forward Brent Ashton. (Above) Philly forward Ilkka Sinisalo is dumped by Quebec player. (Left) The Islanders and Flyers talk things out during final game of their series. Philadelphia eliminated New York and went on to play Quebec for the Wales Conference title. (Opposite top) Oilers' Mark Massier may appear to be yawning but he's actually airing out linesman Gerard Gauthier during Campbell Conference title game in Chicago. The Black Hawks gave Edmonton a bit of a scare by winning Games 3 and 4, but the Oilers won the series in six. (Right) Oilers' Dave Lumley tries to swat airborne puck over Hawk goalie Murray Bannerman.

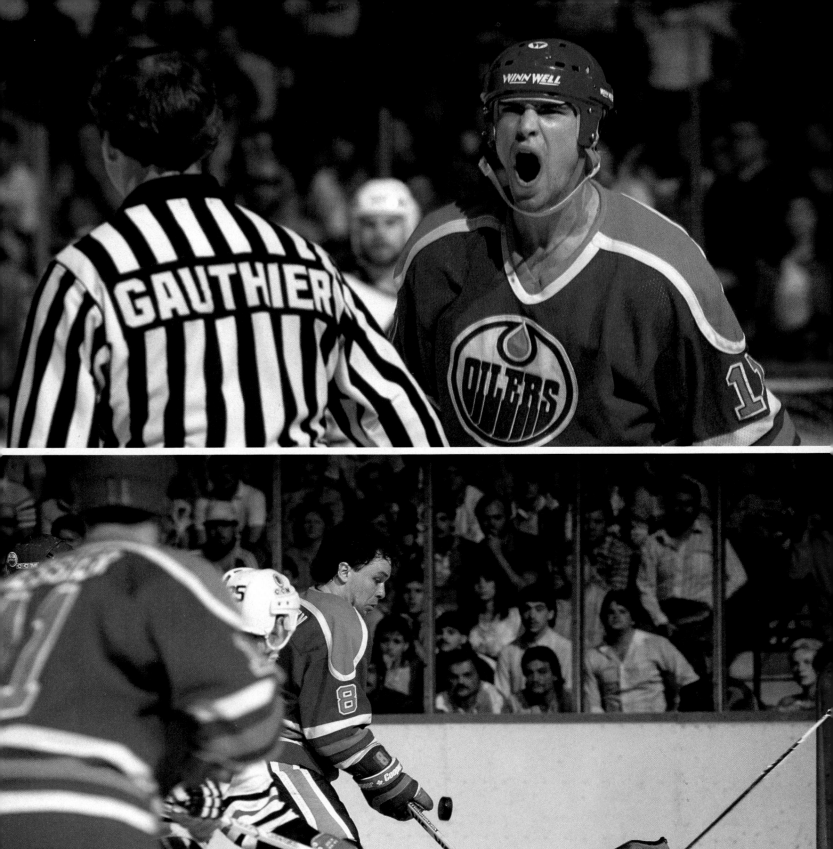

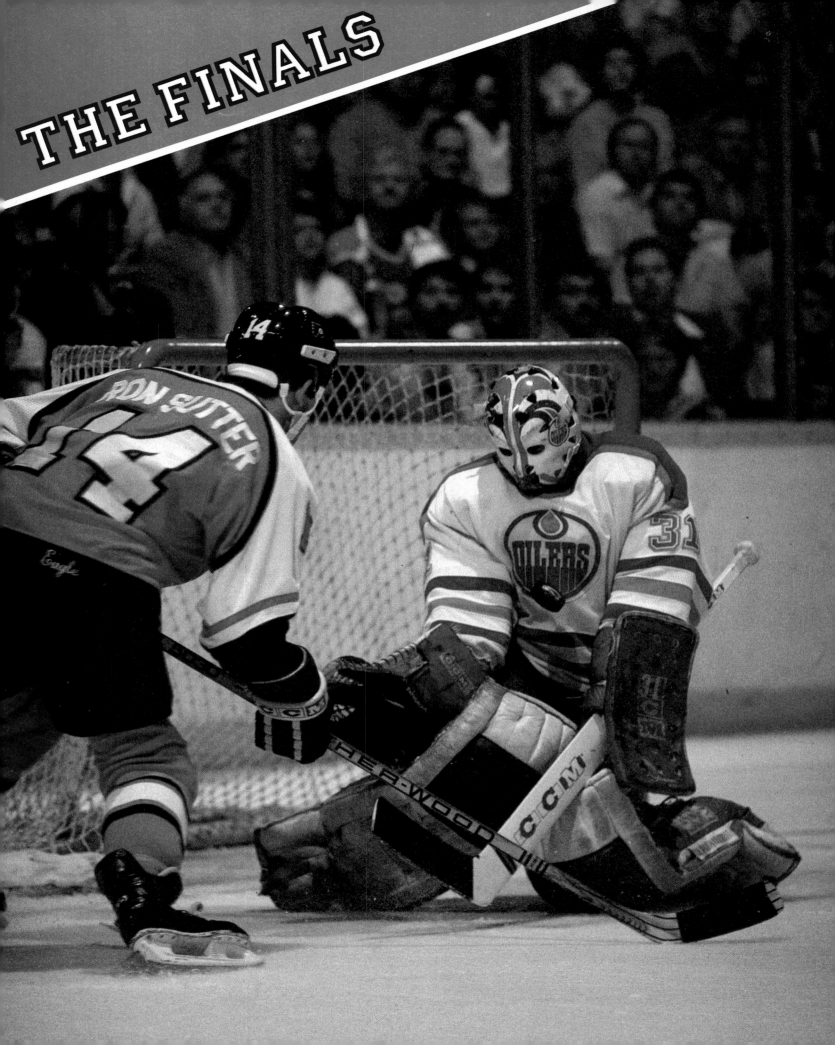

The Oilers eliminated Chicago and went up against Philadelphia (which ousted Quebec) for the 1984-85 Stanley Cup. The series began in Philadelphia where the clubs split the first two games. Upon switching west to Edmonton, the Oilers reigned supreme by a huge margin as they won three consecutive home games to capture the Cup. (Left) Flyers' Ron Sutter is foiled by Oiler goalie Grant Fuhr at close range. Fuhr was brilliant throughout the entire playoffs. His superb performances enabled a sluggish Oiler team to get by Los Angeles in the opening round and he never looked back. Against Philly in the final, he was fantastic - stopping a pair of Flyer penalty shots in Games 4 and 5. Coach Glen Sather felt Fuhr deserved the Conn Smythe trophy as much as Wayne Gretzky.

(Left) Flyers' Brian Propp is hooked around the neck area by Oilers' Lee Fogolin during Game 1 of the Final. (Bottom left) while defenceman Charlie Huddy holds off Philadelphia's Tim Kerr, Flyer rookie Peter Zezel has goalie Grant Fuhr at his mercy. Fuhr, however, was equal to the task and made the save. (Bottom right) after losing the opening game, 4-1, the Oilers battled back to win the second match by a 3-1 score. Here, Paul Coffey congratulates Grant Fuhr before series shifts west to Edmonton.

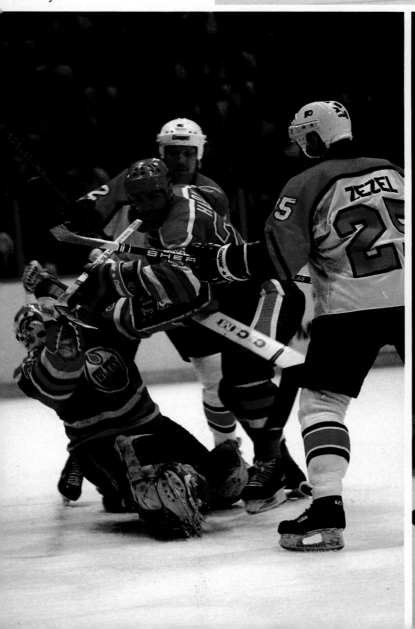

(Opposite top) Flyers and fans whoop it up after Philly goal in Game 1. (Bottom) Referee Kerry Fraser issues warning during scramble in front of net. (Above, top) Flyer captain Dave Poulin leaps for joy after setting up Brian Propp for goal. (Upper, left) Brad Marsh hugs Pelle Lindbergh after Flyers' victory in game 1. (Above) Oilers' Kevin McLelland seems to be checking the time.

(Opposite top) McClelland is hooked by Flyer defenceman Ed Hospodar. (Bottom) McClelland pushes Flyer rookie Peter Zezel (25) out of the way while peering beneath his helmet. (This page, bottom) Flyers' Mark Howe up-ends Quebec's Paul Gillis en route to finals. (Below) goalie Grant Fuhr concentrates on play while Flyers' Derrick Smith (24) tries to distract him from behind. (Right) Oilers' Dave Semenko eyes Flyers' Rich Sutter.

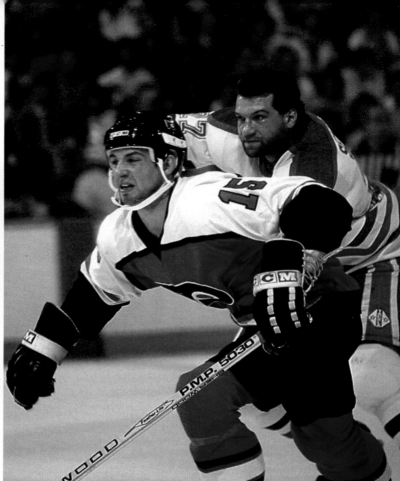

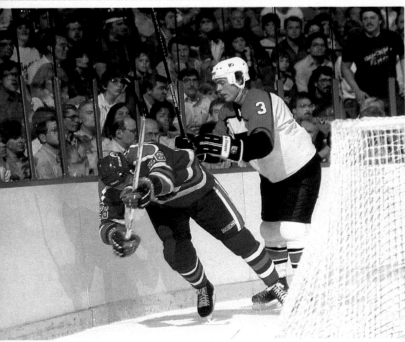

(Opposite top) Flyers' Murray Craven dekes Grant Fuhr out of position but slides puck wide of the net in Game 1. (Left) Fuhr smothers puck with Ilkka Sinisalo hovering over him. (Top) Oilers' Charlie Huddy has lots of open net but Pelle Lindbergh makes the save. (Above) Flyer defenceman Doug Crossman sends Oilers' Mike Krushelnyski to the ice behind the net. (Right) McClelland and Hospodar renew acquaintances.

(Previous page) After Flyers' scoring opportunity is thwarted, both teams head back to ice. (Left) Oilers' Charlie Huddy collides heavily with Rich Sutter in the corner. (Bottom) despite Wayne Gretzky's determined (if not legal) attempt to corral him in flight, Flyer defenceman Mark Howe circles up the ice. (Below) Flyer Murray Craven (32) looks for puck as he pins Oilers' player against the boards. (Right) McClelland and Hospodar just can't seem to get enough of each other!

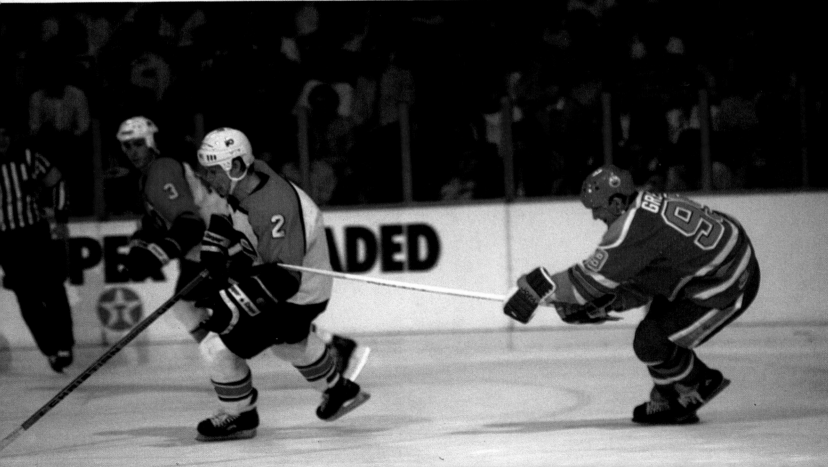

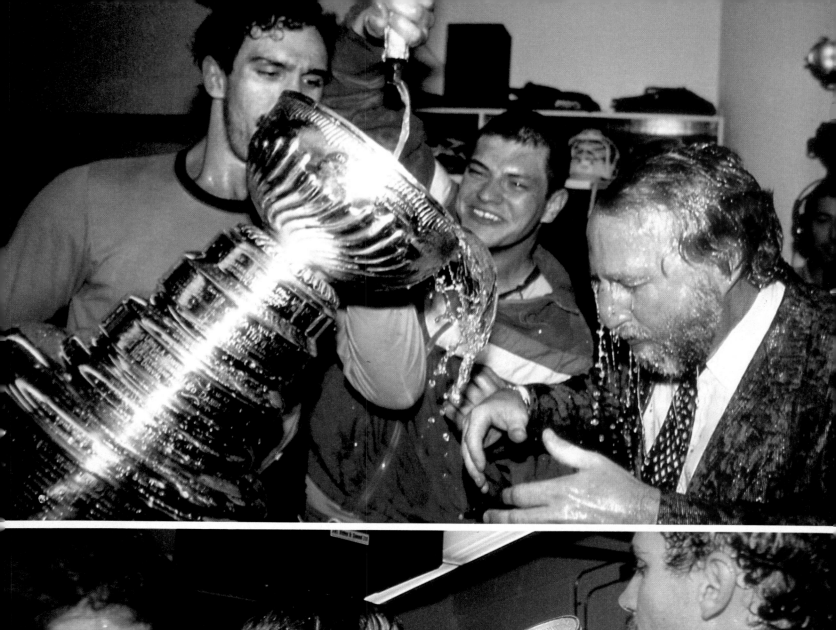

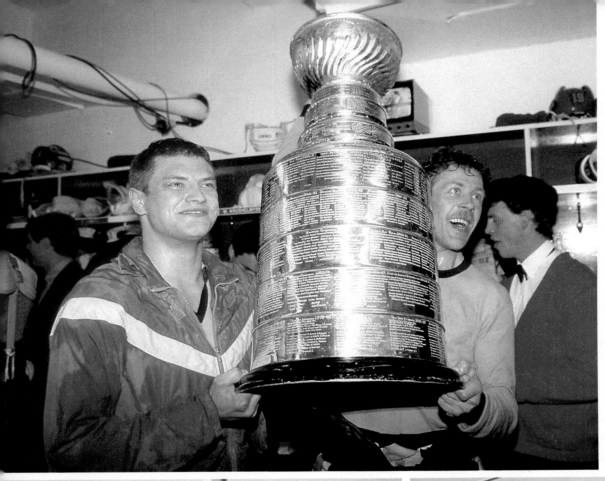

To the victors go the spills (or is that the spoils?). (Opposite top) Oilers' owner Peter Pocklington is doused by champagne as Charlie Huddy holds Stanley Cup. That's Finnish rookie Esa Tikkanen pouring the bubbly. (Opposite bottom) Huddy tips cup so that teammate Mark Napier can swallow a swig of champagne. Napier was the victim of the series' most controversial moment when he was viciously high-sticked in the mouth by Hospodar in Game 3. He lost 3 teeth in the episode. (Left) Tikkanen (the Finn) and Willy Lindstrom (the Swede) pose with coveted Cup. (Bottom left) Winger Jari Kurri who tied an all-time single-season playoff record with 19 goals - relaxes with a brew, a cigar and the Cup. (Bottom, right) Gretzky is joined in celebration by his pal, Joey Moss (right) after winning Cup.

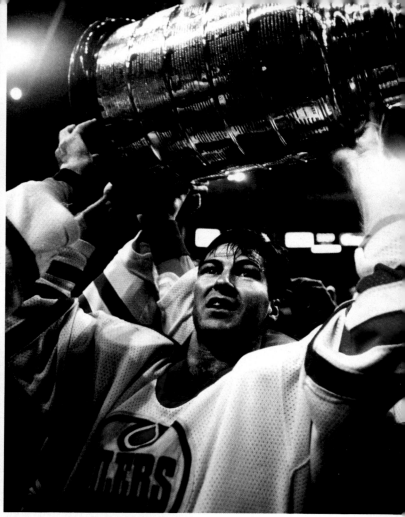

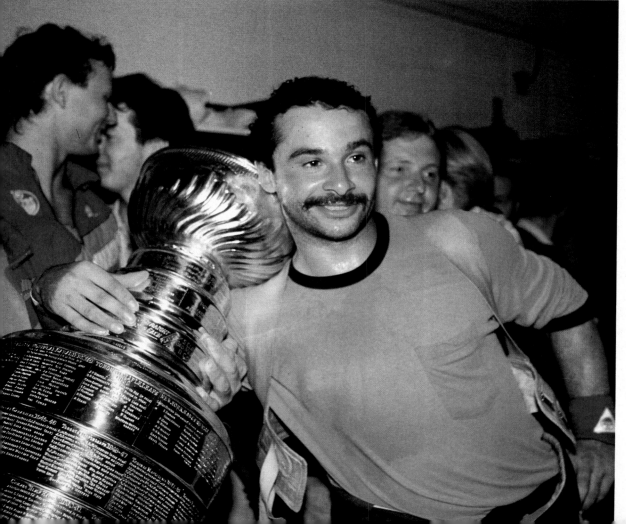

(Above) Willy Lindstrom (left) and Kevin Lowe (right) hoist Stanley Cup over their heads during victory lap at the Northlands Coliseum. A massive crush of photographers and fans made it extremely difficult for the players to move around. (Left) goalie Grant Fuhr poses with the Cup after his splendid performance in the Finals. (Opposite, top) if you're wondering why no one seems to be crowded around Oilers' Glenn Anderson, the reason is rather obvious! Anderson and linemate Mark Messier both played their usual key roles in the Cup triumph. (Far right) sipping merrily on a bottle of bubbly, Gretzky prances past the dressing room mob on his way to the media interview area at Northlands Coliseum. (Right) upon winning the Conn Smythe Trophy, Gretzky said, "In my heart, I wish Paul Coffey's name could go right next to mine." Here, Coffey examines area on Cup that will shortly be engraved with Oiler names.